THE REFERENCE SHELF    VOLUME 41 NUMBER 6

# COMPUTERS AND SOCIETY

EDITED BY

## GEORGE A. NIKOLAIEFF

THE H. W. WILSON COMPANY
NEW YORK          1970

# THE REFERENCE SHELF

The books in this series contain reprints of articles, excerpts from books, and addresses on current issues and social trends in the United States and other countries. There are six separately bound numbers in each volume, all of which are generally published in the same calendar year. One number is a collection of recent speeches; each of the others is devoted to a single subject and gives background information and discussion from various points of view, concluding with a comprehensive bibliography.

Subscribers to the current volume receive the books as issued. The subscription rate is $17 in the United States and Canada ($20 foreign) for a volume of six numbers. Single numbers are $4 each in the United States and Canada ($4.50 foreign).

COMPUTERS AND SOCIETY

Copyright © 1970
By The H. W. Wilson Company

*Standard Book Number 8242-0111-6*

*Library of Congress Catalog Card Number 75-95634*

PRINTED IN THE UNITED STATES OF AMERICA

## PREFACE

To any casual observer of American society in the 1970s computers might seem to be of minor importance. For the most part they are physically out of the public eye. No monumental factories are built to house them. The men who operate them are technicians with none of the distinctive panache of, say, the dedicated professor. The machines themselves, without the sheer mass and power of much of our industrial machinery, seem insignificant toys that hum, click, and flash very discreetly indeed.

What a mistaken view this would be. For computers— machines able to perform a myriad complex mathematical calculations in the space of moments—are the cause and hub of an extraordinary turning point in the civilization we know. It is no exaggeration to say that computers are doing for the mind of man what the introduction and widespread use of machines did for his muscles. By using computers in tandem with machinery and techniques already at his disposal, man now has the potential, for the first time in his long history, of being able to control his destiny.

There is ample evidence of this already. It was with the use of computers that the endless mathematical problems of man's first trip to the moon were solved. Even now computers linked to radar screens watch the frontiers of our nation; the computers can tell the hostile aircraft from the friendly and in that impersonal analysis balance the difference between life and possible destruction.

In subtler ways they reach into our daily lives. In New York City, policemen read the license plates of cars that seem suspicious and a computer—within moments—tells them if the vehicle is stolen or the driver has unpaid traffic fines. At almost any bank in the nation computers register deposits

3

and withdrawals. And at Lordstown, Ohio, General Motors Corporation is using computer abilities to control and manage the making of a car, to see if it can be done more cheaply.

The computer phenomenon is all the more extraordinary because it has come about so swiftly. As recently as the early 1950s the computer was still an intellectual toy, something for academicians to play with and science fiction writers to speculate about. Indeed, it was only in 1951 that the first commercially available automatic computer was delivered. Four years later 1,000 were in operation. By 1965, a decade later, 30,000 were working. By 1975 conservative estimates have it that more than 85,000 will be in use.

In some ways even these numbers are deceptive. Because computers work so quickly, techniques have been developed that allow many users to share them. Thus computer use is proliferating at quantum speeds since almost everyone who wants to (and can afford it) can now plug in and share computer time.

Such abilities of computers—and the future prospects they offer—are not without a darker side. Computer speeds mean quick solutions to statistical or mathematical problems once thought to be too laborious to undertake. These solutions suggest other problems which the computer can then solve just as quickly. The beauty, or the difficulty, of the process is that computers have catapulted man's ability to advance his knowledge from the leisurely pace of working out solutions with pencil and paper to that of the speed of lightning.

This has a profound impact on our society. For, as the solutions are applied directly to work to be done, they tend to eliminate jobs—a process that now goes under the blanket term *automation*. As the process of change quickens, it becomes increasingly difficult for people to understand and absorb the changes. In recent years we have become aware of the phenomenon of the "hard-core unemployed"—usually people of such minimal education and training that they cannot participate in the increasingly sophisticated work process. But there is nothing to guarantee that even people with a modest amount of skill will have jobs five years from now.

Indeed, it is now clear that somewhere in the not too distant future many people may simply not have to work. In some industries, notably the chemical industry, entire processes are already run by computer instructions. How can people, who throughout their lives have believed that to work regularly is good and that to be out of a job is bad, adjust to such a change? What kinds of values are to be substituted for the ones that have served us for centuries?

Such dilemmas breed stresses and fears, not the least of which is the suspicion that the quickly developing machines may learn to think—and then what? To some, such fears may seem absurd. But history reveals that during the industrial revolution rampaging mobs of workers destroyed the machinery they feared so much.

This book is being published near the beginning of this era in which men use computers to expand their knowledge. It answers the basic questions of what a computer is, how it works, and how it came about in the first place. But, perhaps even more importantly, it seeks to put in perspective the enormous impact that the process of accelerating knowledge through computers has had on our society and the impact that this process is likely to have in the future.

The first section of the book notes that we have crossed an invisible line in our technological development, entering a phase characterized by the rapidly expanding use of computers which in turn accelerates the pace of change even more. The second section describes how the computer works. The third deals with the history of events that made computers first necessary and then possible.

The fourth section considers the immediate impact that widespread use of the computer has had on our society. The final section examines some of the less direct but haunting issues and questions that an increasingly computer-oriented future will bring.

The editor thanks the authors and publishers who have graciously permitted their work to be included. Special thanks go to Rosalind Nikolaieff for her help and encouragement while the book was being compiled.

GEORGE A. NIKOLAIEFF

January 1970

# CONTENTS

III.  How Did The Computer Come About?

IV.  The Immediate Impact

V.  The Larger Issues

# I.  DAWNING OF A NEW AGE

## EDITOR'S INTRODUCTION

In the late 1960s there evolved in the United States an extraordinary preoccupation with the future: books were written about it, magazine articles speculated on it, television networks presented special programs attempting to depict it. No one can give any specific reason for the upsurge in interest, but a major factor is that science and technology had suddenly leaped forward, producing inventions and new knowledge at unprecedented rates.

The first article in this section underlines this very rapid advance in science and technology and points out that it has brought man to the verge of control over his destiny. The second article notes that a central factor in the acceleration and explosion of scientific and technological knowledge is the invention of the computer. Most research problems are approached through the scientific method, which essentially means a systematic collection and analysis of data. Properly used, computers are tools that can do this tedious task at speeds far greater than ever before. Accordingly, the article notes, computers are extending man's mind.

The selection that follows is simply a status report on the computer industry as it was at the beginning of 1969. It shows how very quickly computers have been accepted in our society and how their production has grown into a multi-billion-dollar industry.

The next article notes that statistics on the number of computers in use do not tell the whole story. Because of their great speed, computers may be used by many people at virtually the same time. The article thus points out that computer use and application are spreading at a far greater rate than the number of computers in use would indicate.

The fifth selection notes the multitude of ways in which computers are being used and how this is speeding the whole process of technological change, which in turn is causing fears among people whose jobs may be automated away by the machines.

But there's more to the very quick arrival of the computer than proliferating uses for the machines. Because its function is to assist in mental tasks the computer holds a very special relationship to the people its work affects. On balance this relationship, or partnership, is a positive one. The article that follows examines what this partnership is all about and what it may ultimately mean.

This is not to say that the computer has not yet had a vast impact on our lives. It has indeed. It is changing the very fiber of our society, its values, politics, and even interests. The final article in this section looks at some of the trends that have already developed as a result of rapid, technological change and suggests what they may mean.


## THE NEW DIMENSION [1]

What is man's vision of the future? And why today are we so concerned—almost obsessed—with the future?

The reasons are clear. Within recent years we have witnessed an incredible explosion of human knowledge. With that knowledge has come a tremendous increase in the power and influence that human beings can exert over their environment and their fellowmen.

And even more recently, with the realization that we have gained such power and influence, to many has come also the unsettling feeling that all of human destiny is somehow slipping rapidly into man's own hands.

We have been told, as Dennis Gabor, the British physicist, has stated, that we can "invent the future" and the utopians

[1] From "Uneasy World Gains Power Over Destiny," by Glenn T. Seaborg, chairman, United States Atomic Energy Commission. New York *Times.* p C 141+. Ja. 6, '69. © 1969 by The New York Times Company. Reprinted by permission.

among us seize this optimistically to create a glowing vision of man's future. The less optimistic, such as the eminent biologist René Dubos, do not share such a vision.

They agree that man has this newfound power but do not feel he has the wisdom or the ability to use it rationally and constructively to fashion a better future. Still others are more pessimistic, expressing the fear that such power, unwisely used, will lead to man's downfall.

The crux of the matter, whichever side one chooses, is that the degree of power man has gained through his science and technology must be matched by an equal degree of control—control which demands increasingly greater sophistication as well as constant human orientation.

To an extent that we have never known before, we are now faced with the age-old problem that arises when amoral power falls into the hands of moral man. But today this problem is central to our very survival as a species. The science and technology that have brought us this power have always had a way of exposing the raw nerve of truth. Now, directly or indirectly, they have brought us eyeball to eyeball with our environment, our social institutions and the needs, hopes and despairs of all our fellowmen.

How have we arrived at this point? What have man's science and technology done for him—and to him—to give him this incredible new degree of power, and with it this awesome amount of responsibility for determining his future?

Perhaps the answer to these questions lies in the way that man has extended himself beyond his natural evolution. What attributes does this "extended man" have? How has he extended his capabilities, individually and through his society? And where could these and further extensions lead him?

To begin with, let us examine man's extended perception. How far we have come from our dependence on the limitations of our five senses. What an enormous range we have given to these senses through our application of modern science and technology. For contrast, compare some of the perceptive abilities of natural man with extended man. In hearing, natural man cannot detect the frequencies that can be distinguished by a dog nor pick up sounds in an audible range from over a distance of perhaps a few miles. Extended man, however, through modern electronics, can "hear" sounds reproduced from millions of miles in space, from thousands of feet beneath the sea and from any point on the earth.

## Extended Detection

He can detect, and even record and reproduce, the entire range of frequencies definable as sound. He can detect and locate the source of a rumbling earthquake on another continent. He can hear the footsteps of insects in a laboratory bowl, the voices of fish in the sea and even the voices of other humans who may be orbiting the earth or the moon.

Natural man's sense of vision has always been his primary method of knowing about his world. Yet he does not have the acuity of an eagle nor can he adapt to darkness as well as certain nocturnal mammals. His eyes, wonderful as they may seem to him, offer only a very limited picture of his immediate world—or a very immediate picture of his limited world.

But look at extended man: Through scientific innovations which have been developed or refined mainly within the last few decades, he has extended the limits of his sight by such orders of magnitude and in such terms that the very expression *sight* needs redefining.

He is now able to witness indirectly events taking place almost anywhere on earth at the time they happen. He is able to "see" the existence of stars far beyond those he once believed occupied the "outer edges" of space and also to record cosmic events that happened billions of light years ago. He is able to visualize the structure of an atom and to track the paths of its disintegrating particles, though their lifetime be far less than a billionth of a second. He is able to observe life on a microcosmic scale, seeing the detached structure of such simple self-reproducing things as viruses some of which are so small that a trillion of them could fit on the head of a pin. And this same extension of sight inward allows him to study in detail the basic structure of his own living cells and the chemical basis of his heredity.

## New Perspectives

Miraculous as these extensions of man's perceptions are, they are still growing, still adding to his knowledge and power.

For example: Our new earth-orbiting observation satellites offer us an amazing new perspective of our planet—one that can give us much vital information. To natural man a great deal of this information—on his weather, his underground and undersea resources, the condition of his crops, the state of his atmosphere—though literally all around him, remains unobserved and therefore lost to him. But these new satellites, with their new perspective and highly sophisticated sensors, give extended man remarkable new eyes in the sky and the ability to know his planet, its natural systems and resources, as he has never known them before.

At the same time that we have this larger, more encompassing view of the earth and probe farther out into the universe, we are also penetrating deeper into the microcosm.

Every year biochemical research brings us closer to a complete understanding of the code of life and also to the incredible possibility that we may create and control life. New programs in the physical sciences, made possible by the enormous machines—such as the 200 Bev accelerator now under construction in this country—will discover and define even more fundamental forces than we can now record.

And so, the perception of extended man continues to grow. With it also grows his ability to correlate those perceptions into useful knowledge and to communicate them to his fellow extended man. Because it is only through memory and communication that the collective intelligence of extended man grows, it is fortunate that the same scientific revolution which has magnified man's knowledge-gathering ability has given him the electronic tools to handle his growing accumulation of data, to sort it, store it, recall it when he needs it, to solve problems with it, and to some extent put the answers to work for him.

If it were not for these tools, particularly the computer, how would he begin to handle the incredible input of his information explosion, one which in science alone sees the publishing of 100,000 journals a year (in more than sixty languages), a figure doubling every fifteen years?

### The Global Brain

Because of this technetronic ability of extended man to organize and retrieve data so quickly, some see as one possibility for the future a world civilization possessing a computer network the equivalent of a "Global Brain"—one which knows all, recalls all and tells all. Can you imagine the social implications of such a system? . . .

### Has Man Lost Control?

Many thoughtful people believe and fear that the technical civilization we have created is out of hand, that as a macrosystem guided by large economic and social needs and forces, man as such is no longer in control.

In part they base this belief on the idea that efficiency is now a guiding force, that it replaces all human considerations, and that we are also ruled by the notion that whatever is technically possible must be achieved. This thinking leads them to the ideas that we are all becoming cogs in a well-oiled machine and that we will create technological "advances" which will ultimately destroy us—directly or indirectly. Among their examples are nuclear weapons, pesticides, various forms of environmental pollution and genetic and personality control which might be used malevolently.

While I recognize the basis for these people's fears, I do not subscribe to their general theories.

To begin with, I think man has already matured past the point where he will put to use everything he can invent.

He did this primarily at a time in our industrial development when he did not have the ability to foresee the larger outcome of his actions. In spite of the many foolish things we may still do today, I think we are now much more analytical, far-sighted, and wiser than we have ever been, particularly concerning our own survival. Also, we can already see the breakdown of the "cog in the well-oiled machine" theory in much of the rebellion in the world today and a new emphasis on the dignity and growth of the individual.

## Pessimists Illogical

There is much that is illogical in theories of our modern pessimists. For example, would a truly efficient machine be self-destructive?

It seems to me it would be self-adjusting to stresses and strains on its parts since they are vital to its very life, not to mention its efficiency. I think the extreme of these pessimists overlook man's higher instinct for survival as well as his ever-growing awareness of his problems and his ever-increasing ability to deal with them. They themselves are helping us in dealing with our problems, in meeting the challenges of our age, by their "feedback," their warnings and the extent of their alarm over certain mistakes we have made.

But we must not allow ourselves to embrace their despair, to believe that we are caught up in some stream of technologically-guided inevitability. We can help choose our future. There is still choice. There are alternatives. And the more faith we have in our ability to determine our future the harder we will strive to make it a bright one.

## THE BOUNDLESS POTENTIAL [2]

No other technical innovation has changed so many human activities in so short a time. An extension of man's brainpower, it is transforming science, medicine, govern-

[2] From "The Boundless Age of the Computer," by Gilbert H. Burck, member of board of editors of *Fortune* Magazine. *Fortune*. 69:101-10+. Mr. '64. Reprinted by permission of *Fortune* Magazine, © 1964 Time Inc.

ment, education, defense, business. It may transform man himself.

"The electronic computer," says Ray Eppert, president of Burroughs Corporation, "has a more beneficial potential for the human race than any other invention in history." This colossal judgment might seem merely the occupational extravagance of an ardent computer salesman, which Ray Eppert surely is. But the Burroughs chief weighed his words with care, and put the case for the computer no more extravagantly than many a Ph.D. with reservations in his mind and footnotes in his voice. More and more people with special competence in computer circles are coming to the same conclusion.

What, the computer more beneficial than the printing press or the wheel? More than the steam engine or the dynamo and electric motor, to say nothing of atomic power? An impressive case can be made for putting the computer at the top of the list—given the qualification that the latest great technical innovation often exerts the greatest impact because it feeds on previous achievements. The dynamo obviously never would have amounted to so much if a steam prime mover had not existed. The computer itself is classified as a product of the electrical manufacturing industry, and without that industry's tremendous advances it would have remained a challenging but impractical museum piece. A hundred and thirty years ago the functions of the modern computer were understood by a few people; but it remained for the vacuum tube to make the computer practicable, and for diodes and transistors to make it the prodigy it is today.

Certainly no other single item of capital goods has changed the basic terms of so many human activities in so short a time. Within a few years, as the engine of modern information technology, it has profoundly altered the techniques of science, has begun to make government efficient, and has provided a new basis for the strategies of national defense. Above all, it is radically changing business production methods and the art and science of management. Although the machine is the *bête noire* of critics who fear it will accelerate unemployment and compound the worst problems of modern society, it seems destined to shine as a powerful instrument for making business more creative and efficient and hence for raising the nation's real income per person, for eliminating a vast amount of drudgery, and for increasing leisure. In short, for measurably expanding free man's range of choices.

One of the characteristics of the computer that make it unique among technical achievements is that it has forced men to think about what they are doing with clarity and precision. A man cannot instruct the computer to perform usefully until he has arduously thought through what he's up to in the first place, and where he wants to go from there. Even scientists, once they have wrestled with a computer's demands on knowledge and logic, are astonished to discover how much of their mental activity travels in ruts. The rethinking process gets more difficult as the computer gets better. Wherever the machine is used, it is improving enormously the quantity and quality of human cogitation; and it is rapidly becoming a kind of Universal Disciplinarian.

### The Great Processor

Perhaps the best way to explain the machine is to compare it with man himself. In his long and unfinished struggle to master his physical environment, man progressed by processing knowledge. That is to say, instead of relying wholly on his favorite haruspex, or gut reader, he learned to gather and differentiate knowledge, and so to transform it into something useful. It is hardly more than a tautology to observe that practically all the wrong decisions over the centuries, from Darius' attack at Marathon to the birth of the Edsel, have been at bottom the result of insufficient or inadequately processed knowledge. On the other hand, the gods themselves have been on the side of mortals who knew enough not to bother them with everything—who could process knowledge well enough to relate cause and effect and count consequences with tolerable accuracy. Given adequate knowledge, man learned to rely more and more on deductive or analytical judgment, which proceeds from a body of facts, and less and less on guesses and intuitive judgment, which he necessarily uses when a lot of relevant facts are missing.

The electronic computer is basically a device for ingesting, judging, and otherwise processing or usefully modifying knowledge. Thus it enlarges brainpower even as other manmade machines enlarge muscle power. Like man, the computer expresses knowledge in terms of symbols; man's symbols are letters and numbers, and the machine's symbols are electromagnetic impulses that represent letters and numbers. (There are two categories of computers: (1) the analog, which measures and compares quantities in one operation and has no memory; and (2) the digital, which solves problems by counting precisely and sequentially and has a memory. The electric analog computer is about fifty years old, enjoys a big and growing use in simulation and process control, and is "hybridized" with digital computers in some applications. But it accounts for a very small percentage of the market and its potentialities at present are not so catholic as those of the digital machine. Unless this article specifies otherwise, it means digital when it says computer.)

Although man must usually instruct or program the machine minutely, its chief present advantage is that it can manipulate symbols a million times faster than a man with pencil and paper, and can make calculations in a few minutes that might take man alone a century. Richard Hamming of Bell Telephone Laboratories has remarked that the difference between doing a calculation by hand and by computer is the difference between having one dollar and having a million. Sometimes the difference is infinite; only a computer can calculate swiftly enough to analyze the data from a satellite, or to enable man to control the flight of a missile.

But the computer adds more than lightning calculation and fact sorting to man's brainpower. Besides an arithmetic unit, it is equipped with a memory that holds its knowledge on call, a stored program device that follows a set of instructions by code, and control units through which it reads and executes instructions. Perhaps its most portentous faculty is what is called conditional transfer, or sometimes the branch or jump operation, which allows it to choose from alternatives. Without the transfer, the machine must run brutelike through all the alternatives in a given problem to hit the right one; with the transfer, it can *assess* and then *conclude*. In effect, the machine searches its memory and makes judgments and in general acts remarkably like a sentient being. That is how the computer can make selective payroll deductions, and beat the house at blackjack, and why it is indispensable in cybernation, or the process of automatic communication and control.

Most problems presented to computers are algorithmic or "well structured"—that is, problems leading inevitably to a conclusion, such as billing customers, calculating trajectories, or solving equations. But now computer men are trying to make the machine do more. . . . The computer can perform only what we know how to order it to perform. But since it embodies a conditional transfer, suppose we instruct it to learn from experience. Professor Herbert A. Simon of Carnegie Institute of Technology has in effect done just that. He has demonstrated to the satisfaction of a lot of people that he can instruct a computer to solve relatively "ill-structured" problems, which are the kind that infest all life, by using rules of thumb and by trial-and-error search. In the new jargon of computers, Simon has made the machine behave heuristically (serving to discover) as well as algorithmically.

Thus Simon and the other dedicated computer men are writing of machines "which do not merely substitute brute force for human cunning. Increasingly they imitate—and in some cases improve upon—human cunning." Some talk of the immortal brain, or a computer whose external memory store can be expanded indefinitely, to include the wisdom of the ages. This computer would be a paragon of intelligence, able to relate all its stored knowledge accurately, to reason without being corrupted by emotion, to discover new relationships between old things, to solve more of the world's problems than anyone solved before, even to create works of art. Man would be superior to this machine god, the joke goes, only because he presumably could still pull the plug or throw the switch.

Such extrapolations, so uncomfortably reminiscent of the androids of science fiction, have aroused a storm of opposition, and revived in intellectual circles hoary textbook issues like free will vs. determinism and vitalism vs. mechanism. At one extreme are people like Norbert Wiener, a pioneer in computers, who originated the word *cybernetics* and who ... solemnly warns that computers can be improved to the point where they will get out of man's control. At the other are embattled skeptics who denounce the notion that machines can ever really simulate human beings. In between is a group taking various potshots at abuses of the computer, real and imaginary, and at the "dire threat" it presents to employment and the social order....

## A Game for Mental Gear Shifters

The acceptance of the electronic computer, appropriately enough, has been extraordinary, if not unique. Unlike some other great innovations, which have needed anywhere from fifty to one hundred years to assume their role in the scheme of things, it has taken a very big role in a few years, and is headed for a vastly bigger one. A dozen years ago there were fewer than two score machines in the land; today [1964] there are about 16,000 installations; including accessory devices, they are probably worth around $4 billion. Most other great inventions have flourished mainly within single industries; this ecumenically versatile one is already indispensable in most important human activities. Several thousand distinct applications have been cataloged, and the list is out of date before it leaves the presses. Never before, surely, has a single device generated in so short a time so many technical

papers, pamphlets, articles, and books; merely to scan the
daily flow of new and important information about the computer, to say nothing of the bales of quasi-information about
it, is beyond the capacity of anything but the computer itself.
Yet only a small minority of technical experts wholly understand the machine; the vast majority of enlightened laymen
know it mainly as a kind of mysterious twelve-foot refrigerator with blinking lights and whirring tapes. The gulf of in-
comprehension between the experts and laymen is doubtless
far greater than the gulf between Christopher Columbus and
the savage Indians who knelt to worship him on San
Salvador.

And never before, probably, has a single innovation generated such technically sophisticated, talented, competitive,
expansion-minded, well-heeled manufacturing business.
Staffed by thousands of men with advanced degrees, confidently risking billions on research and development, jubi-
lantly peddling machines that embody sensational advances
and yet are almost obsolete by the time they hit the market,
the computer industry is a union of science and business that
makes the auto and appliance industries in their great old
days seem like a bunch of kids playing mumblety-peg. The
game today is surely one for men who know how to shift
mental gears swiftly. If anything is changing faster than
computerized business, it is the business of making computers. About 60 cents of every dollar spent on computer
hardware now goes for the central processor, and the rest
for peripheral equipment like input-output devices, files, and
communications. But in a decade, according to the Diebold
Group, management advisers, peripheral equipment will account for 75 to 80 cents of the hardware dollar. At the same
time, the software or programming business seems to be
growing even faster than the hardware industry; some predict that in seven years software volume will equal hardware
volume.

The industry is dominated and in a way protected by
International Business Machines, which a dozen years ago

in a remarkably skillful shift changed itself from the world's biggest punched-card office-machine company into the biggest electronic-computer company, and one that is always preparing a "sensational" new line. But IBM's competitors, which include such names as Sperry Rand's Univac Division, RCA, GE, Burroughs, Minneapolis-Honeywell, NCR [National Cash Register], and Control Data, are heavily armed with brains, ambition, and money. Their assault on fortress IBM . . . is gathering way as one of the most arresting showdowns of business history.

### To Business, on a Platter

The benefits that the computer has conferred on government and science are tolerably familiar, and may be covered briefly. For government the machine has done something that nothing else has ever done before, at least on a big scale: it has vastly improved the productivity of bureaucracy. In 1951, for instance, the Census Bureau bought a Univac I. By 1960, fortified with several more, the bureau needed only half as many people to do twice the work that 4,500 had done in 1950. The Federal Government, including the Defense Department and the AEC [Atomic Energy Commission], now uses some 1,250 electronic computers, against 730 as recently as 1961, and expects to be using 1,500 or more within two years. However, the computer's contribution to government efficiency doesn't get into the national productivity figures because statistics assume that government output per man-hour remains constant.

To science and technology the computer has of course been a colossal and unprecedented boon. Chemistry, weather forecasts, physics, education, missile design and operation—these are only a few fields in which the machine is responsible for totally new techniques and achievements. Before Bell Laboratories' scientists possessed computers, they spent months building laboratory pilot plants of transmission systems; now they simulate systems by constructing models on paper and running the figures through a computer, and they come up with the ideal system in a matter of days. About 10 per cent of the Laboratories' experiments are performed on the computer, but in time, Richard Hamming estimates, perhaps 90 per cent of them will be.

The combination of World War II and the computer put the military into business in more ways than one. War itself, these days, is only a highly unfriendly kind of business. Of the 800 or more computers operated by the Defense Department, the Air Force employs more than 400. The largest group of these—about 125—manages the Air Force's worldwide inventory, which is worth no less than $12 billion. Computers helped the Air Force Logistics Command to reduce its head count to 146,000 from 212,000 in 1956; and one of the most advanced inventory controls anywhere is its Automatic Resupply Logistic System, which balances inventories by automatically sending out shipping notices whenever the stock of an item anywhere descends to a given level.

Clemenceau, who remarked that war is too important to be left to the generals, would be agreeably amazed by the Air Force's SAGE (semi-automatic ground environment), set up in 1957 to protect the United States from a surprise air attack. Using strategically located computers to interpret information gathered by radar, SAGE automatically identifies and categorizes as friend or foe every craft in the air above the United States and Canada, supplies details of its speed, specifications, location, and physical environment. If necessary, it alerts Air Force planes, assigns targets, or dispatches intercepting missiles. Thus SAGE simulates a large business system with strategically located division offices, all bound together by an information-and-control network. This network, in effect, not only keeps the home office instantaneously aware of regional and system fluctuations in sales, costs, inventories, and profits, but takes the necessary steps to correct imbalances.

### Machines Need Managers

Such military demonstrations of computer ability, together with the research and development done to produce scientific and military systems, have enormously accelerated the business world's acceptance of the computer. In 1954, when experts were estimating optimistically that as many as fifty companies would eventually use computers, General Electric's new Louisville appliance plant took delivery on the first data processor used by a private company, a Sperry Rand Univac. Today the vast bulk of American computers operate in the plants and offices of several thousand companies. Last year alone, U.S. business absorbed more than four thousand, worth nearly $2 billion including peripheral equipment; and the accompanying software cost perhaps another $2 billion. Although a few industry specialists think that business installations will remain on a plateau for a few years while these companies absorb what they've got, others see a steadily rising volume. In any event, all predict that delivered value of business computers will rise sharply in a few years, and even double or triple by the early 1970s.

By no means have all installations to date been unqualified blessings. In a study of more than three hundred installations in twenty-seven major manufacturing companies more than a year ago, McKinsey & Company, the management consultant, found that eighteen of the companies weren't earning enough on the computers to cover their investment, and apparently U.S. business as a whole was making little if anything on them. Overselling was not the basic problem, though doubtless there was some. The main reason for the trouble seems to be that management, particularly top management, did not give enough study and thought to the potential of computers.

The success stories help explain the failures, and why there are steadily fewer failures. Almost invariably the companies that made the machines pay off put computer operation decisions in the hands of senior managers. These men did not look upon the machine as a gift package that needed only to be plugged in, but subjected themselves to its rigorous discipline. They analyzed their businesses and kept looking for new ways to use the computer even when they were employing the machines profitably on routine jobs. They were also willing to reorient their operating routines and their company organizations, if necessary, to exploit the computer. They are the kinds of managers, many are convinced, who will be running U.S. business tomorrow.

The time when executives could fool around with the machine is gone [says one computer-company officer]. Either they make the computer an indispensable part of their business, or they become a dispensable part of business.

This somewhat dogmatic conclusion on the whole seems justified. The machine is developing far more capabilities than anyone dreamed of a few years ago, and no business organization can afford to bypass them summarily. The indefatigably resourceful manufacturers are developing new peripheral equipment, making more tractable machines, finding countless new uses for them, introducing models with startling new powers, and reducing unit costs of using them. And many large users of the machines have taken the initiative and developed applications so original that they regard them as proprietary, and refuse to talk about them.

Most of the profitable operations are still confined to such routine jobs as fulfilling payrolls, making out accounts payable and receivable, and processing insurance data, but even these applications are growing vastly more refined. Thousands of insurance policyholders pay their premiums annually, semiannually, quarterly, monthly; some die, some marry. When billing them, an insurance company's machine has to update information about them. Until recently the data was punched into cards, and the machine had to shuffle through the cards seriati muntil it found the right ones. Now random-access storage devices enable the machine to snatch policy records and extract the information it needs in the twinkling of an eye.

Much more portentous, however, are several sophisticated developments still in their infancy but promising to change business methods radically. One is the information feedback principle, which some regard as one of the world's most important concepts because it governs everything done by individuals, groups, and machines in the process of adjusting to one another. A familiar mechanical example of the principle at work is the common thermostat, where temperature and furnace continually interact to keep heat at a predetermined level.

## Life With the Feedback Principle

Owing in large part to the efforts of Professor Jay Forrester of MIT, the feedback principle is being combined with the computer to create an important management tool. The computer's great role here is to eliminate delays in communication; in an automated oil refinery, for example, hundreds of measuring devices lead to the machine. The computer, having been given thousands of instructions on how to react to the readings of the measuring devices, *instantaneously* applies heat or pressure or otherwise adjusts the controls. Because it keeps on reacting and making adjustments instantaneously, it never has to make large adjustments.

And so with inventories, which are a prime problem for both corporations and the economy. To show how difficult it is to keep stocks in line with demand, computer people like to play an inventory game. In its simple form, several people participate. One represents a retailer, two represent distributors, and a fourth the factory warehouse manager. Others represent customers and the factory. When goods are bought by the customers, a chain of events is begun that ends in the factory the equivalent of five weeks later. The game quickly fouls up. Owing to the long lead time, retailers, distributors, and warehouse managers misjudge their needs because they don't know what happens until some time after it has happened. They find themselves with either insufficient or excessive inventories. Thus a tiny disturbance at the sales end results in a big dislocation at the factory. In real life the inevitable adjustment proves very expensive. Ill-adjusted inventories, for individual companies, result in high costs or worse; for the economy as a whole, excessive inventories usually result in recession, which in its majestic impartiality hits companies that have managed to keep their inventories in line—though not nearly so hard as those that haven't.

Owing in part to computers, significantly, modernized inventory management has already had a stabilizing effect on the economy. The national ratio of inventory to stocks has not changed much over the years, but many businesses, notably auto dealers, must carry larger stocks to afford wider ranges of choice; in other words, better inventory control has enabled manufacturers to offer better service without increasing costs and risks. So although relatively few companies are yet using advanced inventory systems, restraint in inventory buildup is one of the strongest supports of the economy's current salubrity. What might happen when all big companies use computers to control inventories is an exhilarating speculation.

Another portentous development is simulation. Note that the inventory game, by simulating a real inventory system, allows the players to study its faults and correct them with computers. In much the same way, simulation is being applied to management problems. Professor Forrester, using one minute of computer time, has simulated the operation of an entire business over a period of four hundred weeks. In real life, a description of a company's operations is fed into the computer, which produces several alternatives for decisions about financial, manpower, product-flow, and other operating factors. From these alternatives, management merely has to choose the best ones. In planning new service stations, for example, some oil companies estimate profitability by simulating two or three years of operation at proposed sites, and so eliminate most if not all the guesswork in their planning.

Ken Powell, IBM's manager of educational research, says that every application of a computer is a simulation; properly understood, it provides unique insights into business. Companies are catching on. What often happens, says Powell, is that a businessman starts with a payroll job whose purpose is merely to get the checks to his employees. He begins to see how the computer can be used to analyze distribution and manufacturing, and then how it can do routine inventory work. Next it dawns on him that in programming the computer to do certain jobs, he must in effect set up models of parts of his business. In the end he finds himself making experimental models of his company's activities. From these he can make decisions about them that he could have made no other way; instead of relying on guesses and intuition, he now can go ahead on logical deductions from facts.

Finally, there are new methods of scheduling work such as Program Evaluation and Review Technique (PERT) and the Critical Path Method (CPM) .... Suffice to say here that these time- and money-saving systems are proving highly popular and that without computers they would be impossible; moreover, they, like some of the other techniques we have discussed, use the machines heuristically.

Such are some of the commercial avenues down which computers are leading. As yet, these avenues have not joined in the construction of the "total" system about which some computer men descanted so persuasively a few years ago. A total system, as the name suggests, would be one in which all a company's inputs and outputs are automatically coordinated. Orders would result in the appropriate allocations of labor and materials, and inventories would be appropriately adjusted. Payments and bills would be mailed. Markets would be gauged, and managers would have only to read the tape and make key decisions. Perhaps the nearest thing to a total system is SAGE; but business is much more complex than cold war, and it may be a while before the business equivalent of SAGE is working.

Meantime, there is plenty to be done in making use of existing techniques and systems. John Diebold, whose group has advised many firms on automation, insists that most companies have yet to realize what is happening to the handling of information in a business. "In some companies," he says, "this will mean a change in methods; in others, a change in the whole core of the business."

### The "General Problem Solver"

Since the machine can guide and fortify and even make some decisions, what will it do to the men who now make the decisions? The computerized executive world twenty years from now is a special interest of Herbert Simon, who was a political scientist specializing in administrative behavior when the computer was a cloud on the horizon. Simon takes the viewpoint that executive decision making is analogous to the behavior of the computer. He therefore divides it into (1) solving programmed or well-structured problems; and (2) solving nonspecifically programmed or ill-structured problems. Examples of the former: clerical and other routine jobs such as ordering office supplies, pricing orders by catalog, and working out payroll deductions—plus a long list of somewhat less repetitive jobs such as balancing assembly lines, determining the product mix for an oil refinery, planning manufacturing and employment schedules, and even choosing trust portfolio investments. Examples of nonspecifically programmed problem solving: consequential decisions for which there is no exact precedent, such as a general's decision to attack, or a company manager's to mount a sales campaign.

Mathematical techniques and the electronic computer have already revolutionized the whole business of routine programmed decision making. Now they are pushing into many middle-management decision areas, such as those in manufacturing and warehousing. Before long, Simon says, they will make most of a company's programmed decisions, just as they will control manufacturing operations. But as big a revolution, he predicts, will occur when heuristic techniques enable the computer to make more nonspecifically programmed decisions, which are the kind on which the experienced manager exercises his judgment and intuition. A good example of decision making or problem solving on the heuristic borderline is the prevailing practice of assigning computers instead of engineers to modify the designs of standard electric motors according to the customers' specifications. When the order comes in, the computer searches through its memory, finds the right design, and modifies the design to fit the need.

In more complex decision making, such as deciding on company strategy, ill-structured problems must be broken down into goals or subgoals, and means must be related to ends. Simon, together with his associates Allen Newell and J. C. Shaw, in projects sponsored by Rand Corporation and Carnegie Tech, has done a lot of work in analyzing complex problem solving and in instructing a computer to perform accordingly. The *chef d'oeuvre* of the three men is what they call a General Problem Solver, or a set of instructions that frees the computer from the rigidities of ordinary programs. This GPS, they claim, enables the machine to behave adaptively, to reason in terms of means and ends, to solve problems by first solving subproblems, and to "adjust aspiration to the attainable." Using the GPS principle, Geoffrey P. E. Clarkson of MIT has successfully simulated a trust-investment officer (*Portfolio Selection: A Simulation of Trust Investment*, Prentice Hall).

## *"Centralized Decentralization"*

Regardless of what happens in heuristics, computer men predict, jobs at the middle-management level will become more specialized, specific, and highly programmed; they will also become fewer. On the other hand, managers at the top levels, freed of the need for analyzing details, will more than ever require the faculties of innovation, creativeness, and vision. The computer, precisely because it will make all relevant information instantly available to top management, will mean more centralization; the phrase in computer circles is "centralized decentralization." Owing to teleprocessing, or the integration of all corporate outposts with the central office (as in SAGE), centralization will be a simple matter.

All information will be "on line" or sent directly into a computer as soon as it is born; the whole operation will be "real time"—that is, data will be processed and fed back into the machine to control each "situation" as it develops.

Such developments, many argue, will tend to humanize rather than dehumanize business. The company man, the Organization Man, will still exist, but only to the extent that he does or ever did exist. The kind of large-scale organization that the machine will encourage should encourage personal initiative. At the average worker's level the machine, because it continually reports back on a job, is already improving his sense of personal participation.

> Constant monitoring [says William Norris, founder and president of Control Data Corporation, which uses one of its own management systems] makes employees feel part of the team effort, because their performance is judged without bias. We've found that people consequently upgrade their own performance.

At the middle-management level, Simon argues, much time is now taken up with pacesetting, work pushing, and expediting. As decision making becomes automated and rationalized, these functions are likely to become less important. The manager will deal with well-structured problems, and won't have to spend so much time persuading, prodding, rewarding, and cajoling "unpredictable and sometimes recalcitrant people." Some managerial types, he admits, get a lot of satisfaction out of manipulating personal relationships; but he believes the diminution in general frustration, for middle managers as a group, will more than offset the other loss.

Heuristically programmed computers, Simon predicts, will be a long time surpassing men on jobs where they exercise their senses and muscles as well as their brains—i.e., running a bulldozer over rough ground, examining a piece of tissue in medical diagnosis, face-to-face service jobs, and so on.

> Man has an advantage in rough environment [he explains]. Who would be easier to automate—the theoretical physicist or the experimental? The theoretical. The experimental physicist still

has to cope with outside environment, whereas the theoretical one deals with concepts, ideas, and other inputs that have been highly processed.

Relative costs, in the last analysis, will decide who does the job; if a decision-making computer comes to $10,000 a month, it obviously would cost more than three middle managers. As yet, computers put to heuristic problem solving do not have anything remotely like the advantage over man that they boast in arithmetic and scientific computing. But the unit costs of using a computer are declining steadily.

### "Changes Have Got to Be Made"

The realization that the computer may be able to do a lot a man can do has accelerated the uproar about unemployment, in certain quarters, to panic proportions. Fevered by vague premonitions about the long-range consequences of the computer, many social pundits are discharging pneumatic predictions about how the machine will plow up the whole order. The consensus of a high-level symposium at . . . [the 1963] convention of the American Federation of Information Processing Societies seemed to be that the computer would be a large factor in making relatively full employment hard to achieve.

Most pessimistic of the lot was W. H. Ferry, vice president of the Fund for the Republic, director of its Study of the Economic Order, and a man given to looking into the future farther than the human eye can see. It is Ferry's oft-stated thesis that the United States is caught on a horn of plenty, and that economic theories adequate to the old industrial revolution are no longer good enough. Since the individualism of the eighteenth and nineteenth centuries and "old theories of private property" are casualties of technology, Ferry argues, the complexity of the scientific-industrial state calls for more and more national planning.

These machines are ingenious but not necessarily important [said Ferry at the computer symposium]. Our sociopolitical thinking is still back in agrarian days. Changes have got to be made.

This kind of thinking, like King Lear's threats to do such things as "What they are, yet I know not, but they shall be the terrors of the earth," gets considerably ahead of the facts in the short run, and woefully distorts the possibilities over the long run. Social change is nothing new. In the main, social progress, as it is measured today, is a result of rising productivity. If output per person remains constant or declines, all that governmental power can do is to distribute poverty more evenly. Rising productivity, because it changes the relative value of jobs, produces most if not all significant social changes. . . . The critical question, obviously enough, is whether the computer will help accelerate the present rate of productivity growth so explosively that the economy will be unable to absorb people as fast as they are displaced.

Despite spectacular individual examples of the computer's ability to displace people, it seems to have had little effect on the nation's aggregate productivity—so far. Although productivity in the private economy has grown at about 3.5 per cent annually for three years now, against an average of 2.5 per cent in the seven previous years, similar spurts have occurred in the precomputer past. And what is often disregarded is that the economy is showing a gratifying ability to create jobs. It is true that U.S. manufacturing employment hardly increased at all in the past four years, while manufacturing output rose 18 per cent; but in the same years other employment, despite a brace of rolling recessions, expanded enough to elevate total employment from about 65.6 million to about 68.8 million. In 1963 alone, when rising productivity in effect subtracted about two million jobs from the economy, nonfarm wage and salary employment increased by more than 1.5 million. In other words, the economy in effect created a total of more than 3.5 million jobs, and practically all were provided by private enterprise. *Fortune's* Roundup estimates that if GNP [Gross National Product] rises to $650 billion (in late 1963 prices) by the middle of 1965, unemployment will be approaching "normal" levels, and the economy may absorb nearly all the employables. The unemployables, particularly the unskilled, will of course remain the problem.

The doomsday prophets ignore this. The moment of truth, they keep insisting, is still to come, and it will come all of a sudden. Their arguments run like this:

1. Computer applications have not yet affected national employment figures partly because their ability to displace people has been temporarily offset by more jobs in computer manufacturing and in new installations. Much heavy initial expense is charged to current account, which tends to hide the rate at which productivity improves. But soon the development phase will be over.

2. What intensifies the grim outlook is that the computer's great impact will come at a bad time. The labor force, owing to the wartime baby boom, is increasing at a net rate of around a million a year, and by the end of the decade will increase by nearly two million a year. Owing to computerized automation and cybernation, the number of blue-collar jobs is likely to increase little if at all; and one has only to look at the computer's successful routine applications to see what it may do to white-collar employment.

3. The computer indirectly spurs productivity. Not only does it make existing machines more productive, but it stimulates the purchase of newer and still more efficient machines, thus compounding its threat to employment.

### Millions of New Jobs

These points are apposite and worth attention, and therein lies their potency in debate. But they are only one side of the story. Computers are not made out of thin air, and emphatically they do not operate unattended. The computer industry, including the infant software business of processing information for the computer, is employing more and more people. Paul Armer, of RAND Corporation, estimates that it will create a million new jobs in the next five years.

Some say that programming alone will employ 500,000 by 1970.

The key factors are payoff and total investment. Just as the importance of any machine to the economy may be roughly gauged by the amount of capital invested in it, so its disemployment effect may be roughly gauged by the net return on that capital. Last year, as already noted, U.S. government and industry bought or leased computers and accessory devices worth almost $2 billion, and in five years may be spending two or three times as much. These outlays are great, but they are a small part of the roughly $80 billion that industry and government will be investing in the private economy this year; five years from now they will still be a relatively small part of the money government and industry will be investing then.

Assume that computer users will eventually save a staggering 50 per cent annually on the capital value of their equipment, a margin the average user won't remotely approach for a long time. Five years hence, on annual hardware shipments valued at some $4 billion, they would earn some $2 billion, which could be equated with perhaps 200,000 fewer jobs. Or to be safe, double the number. But remember that in 1963 alone the economy in effect created a total of more than 3.5 million jobs.

Such reckoning, it is true, takes no account of the fact that the computer pervades so many activities and makes so much other capital equipment more productive. But the disemployment effect of all other plant and equipment, some of it automated and computerized, may also be measured roughly by its payoff. An uncontrollable upward surge in unemployment would necessarily be accompanied by a huge increase in payoff, and the expectation of the payoff would be generating a colossal boom in capital spending. The steel industry is a case in point. It has far more than enough capacity, but it is spending huge sums on oxygen converters and automatic mills because it believes they will pay off handsomely. If all industry were anticipating similar payoffs, U.S. capital investment today probably would be vastly greater than it is.

## The Timely Replenishment

What is too often forgotten is that machines immemorially have not merely replaced men, but freed them to do other things, and so enlarged consumers' range of choices. The cause and effect relationship between displacement by the machine and the creation of new jobs is hard to trace, but it has always been there. It still is there. The computer, too, will indirectly help create new jobs. A computer-controlled oil refinery employs fewer people than a conventional refinery, but it helps bring costs and prices down; and a steady reduction in the real price of petroleum products helps increase the demand for them and so generates thousands of jobs in their distribution and sale. An automated plastics plant creates jobs for managers, engineers, salesmen, manufacturers, retailers. Sometimes, moreover, productivity increases are "hidden" in the form of a product's improved quality and utility. Thanks in part to computers in factories and offices, today's automobile is a much better car than previous models costing the same; thanks to computer-guided inventory controls, the consumer has a wider range of choice in cars than he has ever had before.

An excellent case could be made for the proposition that if the computer did not exist, it would have to be invented. Only a few years ago a good many economists were wondering whether U.S. productivity could keep on rising as it rose in the early postwar years, and some were skeptical when in 1959 *Fortune* projected an average annual increase of about 3 per cent for the 1960s. Their skepticism was hardly whimsical. Ever since the original industrial revolution, the per capita growth rate of nations has been the result not of a single development but of a series of developments. As one innovation began to exhaust its power to multiply human effort, another came along. In many U.S. industries, such as agriculture, mining, and some manufacturing, there were portents of such exhaustion. In others featherbedding was (and still is) rife. The big question was not job displacement, but what would provide a new lift to the per capita growth rate. The answer to the question appears to be the computer. It will doubtless go down in history not as the scourge that blew unemployment through the roof, but as the technological triumph that enabled the American economy to maintain and gradually increase the secular growth rate on which its greatness depends.

## THE OVERNIGHT SUCCESS [3]

The ever-onward march of the computer seems to have joined death and taxes as one of mankind's few certainties.

New applications, new industries and, of course, new installation, sales and production records were created by the electronic computer in 1968.

More of the same will occur in 1969 and as far forward as most trained eyes can see.

While the computer industry is sprinting toward new achievements, it has also begun a much-needed stabilization process. This is not to say that the industry has settled down, far from it, but only that its characteristics are beginning to be defined.

It is now apparent that the computer business has become a number of interrelated industries with an overall framework of electronic data processing.

### New Industries

General purpose computer manufacturers, special purpose computer makers, peripheral equipment companies, software concerns, service bureaus, consultants, equipment

[3] From "Computer Business Races On," by William D. Smith, staff reporter. New York *Times*. p C 85. Ja. 6, '69. © 1969 by The New York Times Company. Reprinted by permission.

leasing concerns, data banks and time-sharing activities have all become industries in their own right.

In the years to come some will become truly giant industries.

The computer business is the world's fastest growing major industry, no matter what measuring tape is used. The fact that the International Business Machines Corporation, with a market worth $42 billion, is the world's most highly valued security, is indicative of what Wall Street thinks of the industry's future.

Yet in 1956 only 570 computers were installed in the United States with a total market value of $340 million. At the close of last year worldwide installation of computers totaled some 70,000 machines, with a purchase value of well over $20 billion.

Of the worldwide total some 56,000 are installed in the United States. Approximately 14,300 were installed last year, according to the Diebold Group, a management consulting organization specializing in automation.

### Machine Sales Up 15 Per Cent

Sales of computer hardware, or machines, rose more than 15 per cent to about $7 billion in 1968 and a comparable increase is expected this year.

The market for software, the programs needed to make the machines perform the desired tasks, hit about $6 billion in 1968, according to the *EDP* [Electronic Data Processing] *Industry Report,* a well-informed trade newsletter. This figure is expected to increase by at least 20 per cent this year and reach $11 billion in 1972. If it lives up to expectations, its size and importance will exceed that of hardware in the next decade.

The more than 1,000 data-processing service bureaus across the United States grossed about $700 million last year and are expected to grow 40 per cent this year.

Sales of such peripheral equipment as card readers and printers rose to about $3 billion last year.

## PLUGGING IN [4]

There is little doubt about the brilliance of the computer. It has, as promised, become a marvelously versatile tool.
It can judge stresses in a bridge design, draw up payrolls,
calculate a missile trajectory, and check a credit rating—all
in fractions of a second. But the man who asks the questions
may wait hours or days as replies calculated at the speed of
light filter back to him through layers of experts and office
routine. The office bureaucracies enveloping most computers
frustrate the user and limit the utility of the computer for
problems that require immediate answers or a running dialogue between the computer and the man. "Real-time" in-
timacy has been possible only by devoting one high-speed
computer exclusively to one slow-thinking human, a waste-
ful and prohibitively costly way of employing computers for
most practical purposes. Now direct access to computers and
a "real-time" dialogue are evolving through the technique
called time-sharing—one of the most important developments
in the use of computers since the first machines were made
twenty years ago.

Time-sharing distributes computer services at truly computerized speeds. It provides a number of users with direct
access to a single computer simultaneously and remotely so
that each has the illusion of having exclusive machine time.
Like a master chess player facing many opponents, the computer switches from one user to the next, though at intervals
measured in milliseconds. And since the time is shared, so
is the cost, which puts an expensive computer within reach
of a modest budget.

A concept born of the frustration of computer programmers in the 1950s and developed primarily on university
campuses in the early 1960s, time-sharing is now becoming
solidly established in the computer market. Time-sharing
services now account for only $15 million to $20 million a

[4] From "Computer Time-Sharing—Everyman at the Console," by Jeremy
Main, associate editor of *Fortune* Magazine. *Fortune*. 76:88+. Ag. '67. Reprinted by permission of *Fortune* Magazine, © 1967 Time Inc.

year in business, according to one estimate, but by the 1970s
they could account for at least half of the multibillion-dollar
computer business. There are so many brilliant young engineers and mathematicians carrying time-sharing forward
in so many places, in so many directions and with such pro-
fusion of theory, that the only certainty about the growth of
time-sharing is that it will be fast. And like any technology
advancing under ardent pressure, it is taking false steps—as
several major manufacturers hungering after new markets
have discovered.

There are computers specially designed for time-sharing,
but modifications to an ordinary computer will do. The
physical alterations, by the exotic standards of the industry,
are relatively simple. Some additional equipment is needed.
For instance, the time-sharing computer needs a traffic
switchboard, which is often another smaller computer, to
receive the large number of messages coming in simultaneously and to transmit the replies back to the users. A time-
sharing system also needs large memories on drums, disks,
and tapes to store the programs and data of many users.

However, far more important than any of these hardware
items, a time-sharing computer requires an "executive" or
"control" program. Unlike a standard computer, which simply carries out instructions for a single job, the time-sharing
computer is required to supervise the work demands of some
thirty to sixty users (and many more in the future) who
have different kinds of problems to solve in a variety of different computer languages. The executive keeps the whole
system running efficiently and in a sequence determined by
priorities. It assigns actual computing time among its many
users, say 200 milliseconds for each client on line. If a client's
problem is not solved within the time limit or "quantum,"
the executive may set it aside in a temporary memory, go on
to queries of other users, and then return to the unsolved
problem. The executive fetches the client's data or programs
out of storage, and puts them back there once the client is
finished. It also can prevent one user from interfering with

the program of another and altering it or wiping it out—a facility that goes by the technical name of "memory protection." It keeps a record of who uses the machine, makes corrections, even gives helpful hints to unskilled users, and performs hundreds of other housekeeping duties. When all goes well, the executive works so swiftly that any individual user is unaware he is sharing the computer with others.

## Thinking for Itself

The difference between the speed of a computer and the sluggishness of a man typing at one of its terminals allows the executive to provide each customer with a reply almost as soon as his question is transmitted, or at least within seconds if the computer should, at that time, be overworked. The executive—the critical item of software in a time-sharing system—is an enormously complicated set of instructions permanently stored in the high-speed core memory of the computer. It is the guts of time-sharing—an elaborate master program that is extremely difficult to write. In effect it can make a machine, which can only do what it is told to do, act as if it could think for itself.

The significance of time-sharing is illustrated best by the changes in the way the computer is used, rather than by changes in the computer itself. By the batch method of computer processing, which is still the most common system in use, the computer handles one problem at a time. Each job is taken to a human programmer, who formulates it in computer language, writing the program, which is then punched on cards. The cards are carried by hand to the computer center and put into an in-box. When a batch of cards has accumulated, they are "read" onto magnetic tape, which a tape handler feeds to the computer. The problem itself is usually solved in seconds, and then data is poured out by a high-speed printer. But the user does not see his answer for a while yet. It comes back to him down the bureaucratic pipeline, and after hours or days of waiting, his answer may easily be that the problem was programmed incorrectly. If so, the whole elaborate procedure must be repeated in a "debugging" operation and a rerun that probably again takes only a few seconds of computer time.

In contrast with such tedious procedures, time-sharing permits the user to deal directly with the computer. He sits down at a console like a typewriter in his office, laboratory, home, or wherever, dials the computer as he would dial a telephone number, and then types out his questions. There are no layers of people or processes to slow him down; he is addressing the computer directly and the answers come back directly—printed out on his own machine.

This immediate contact between the user and the computer speeds up service, but it also gives computer work an exciting new quality known unexcitingly as "real-time interaction." It frees the user from having to set up formal questions and, in due course, getting formal answers, as in the batch method. Instead he has a direct dialogue with the computer. He can ask unplanned questions that occur to him during the dialogue and were not foreseen in the program, or he can alter the framework of the problem while it is being solved. Interaction also means that many users can work together, or build on joint data files or programs, through their common computer. It also means the capacity to "debug" a new program quickly because the "bugs" become immediately evident. It makes the batch system look ponderous and limited.

Real-time interaction permits doctors at Mary Hitchcock Hospital in Hanover, New Hampshire, to treat uterine tumors with a degree of scientific accuracy previously impossible without monopolizing a whole computer. Doctors have had to guess how much radiation was being administered to vulnerable organs near the uterus in the course of treating a tumor; they could not make precise calculations relating the strength of the radiation to the other organs. At the hospital now, the radiation department has a console linked to Dartmouth College's time-sharing system at the other end of the campus. When the radiation applicator is in position, the radiologist takes an X-ray, feeds the computer the coordinates for the positions of the applicator and the vulnerable organs. The computer tells him in an instant precisely how rapidly the dose is accumulating in each organ, thereby determining the safe limits of exposure to the radiation. The radiologist —when he could get away—used to take his data over to a batch-process computer. Sometimes he had to wait hours before he had his answers and at best it took an hour.

The list of current and possible uses grows faster than the technology. The Pentagon may use a time-sharing system to play war games, or to have instant reference to airfield characteristics or conditions, or for any number of other analytical or reference uses. Graduate students at MIT, undergraduates at Dartmouth, and students in a number of New England public and private high schools have already acquired the habit of casual reference to computers from convenient consoles. General Electric and the Cambridge problem-solving firm of Bolt, Beranek & Newman, Inc. have designed a hospital and medical information-processing system known as MEDINET. It can find an empty bed for a new patient, tell a ward nurse what medications to give, and make up a patient's bill, to name only a few of its functions.

Dr. J. C. R. Licklider of MIT and IBM, a pioneer of the time-sharing concept, talks of developing an "on-line intellectual community" of specialists with overlapping interests working together, building on each other's stored programs and data. With the knowledge they could share as a community, they may be able to diminish "the feeling of incompetence" that afflicts a man working alone with a computer when he realizes how little he can accomplish in a lifetime. In the government, on the campus, and in business there are already experiments and plans for great networks of time-shared computers. The Defense Department's Advanced Research Projects Agency, for example, is asking the managers of seventeen time-sharing systems across the country that it has helped to arrange to tie themselves together into an experimental network.

Even among time-sharing enthusiasts, there are critics who think the visionaries are going too far. Huge, multipurpose networks or "utilities" of computers, the doubters say, will become unmanageable monsters, spending so much of their computing effort keeping house that they will have little energy left to do actual problem-solving work. The executive could become so elaborate that it could itself be the principal consumer of the calculating power of the computer, an event that has occurred in some systems under development. Elmer C. Kubie, president of Computer Usage Company, Inc., of New York, who believes time-sharing has been overrated, says:

The more universal such a thing becomes, the more ponderous and inefficient it becomes. The system devotes significant time to administering and keeping track of itself rather than providing service to the user. I call this activity introspection.

### The Beginnings at MIT

It was during the late 1950s, when the hardware of electronic computers first became routinely operational, that the idea of time-sharing began to develop. The impulse came mostly from the frustration that developed among scientists and programmers bottlenecked by the batch-processing system. It was a British mathematician, Christopher Strachey, who, at a UNESCO congress in 1959, gave the first public paper on time-sharing. That same year Professor John McCarthy, now of Stanford, wrote an internal memorandum distributed at MIT. The two men had worked independently and were the first to go on record with specific solutions to the problems of time-sharing. Serious research began at MIT, where Professor F. J. Corbató developed what has since become, in Project MAC (for machine-aided cognition or multiple-access computer), one of the most advanced time-sharing systems now at work in the country. The idea of time-sharing spread to other colleges, notably Dartmouth and Carnegie Tech.

The honors for the first demonstration of time-sharing went to the MIT Computation Center in November 1961, when four "remote" consoles in the same room were hooked, briefly, into an IBM 709 vacuum-tube computer. The following September, Bolt, Beranek & Newman in Cambridge began time-sharing on a Digital Equipment Corporation PDP-1. In May 1963, the System Development Corporation, an offshoot of the RAND Corporation, made its first tests of time-sharing in Santa Monica, and in May 1964, Dartmouth, with GE equipment, joined the time-sharers at four o'clock one morning. "It was pretty crude," says Dr. Thomas E. Kurtz, who directs Dartmouth's Kiewit Computation Center. "It didn't work for five minutes without stopping."

In 1962, Dr. Licklider, a versatile, articulate psychologist, was invited to Washington to join the Advanced Research Projects Agency. After Licklider's arrival, Federal funds began to flow from ARPA, and time-sharing became a serious proposition. Project MAC was established at MIT under Professor Robert M. Fano with a $3 million annual budget supplied by ARPA. The agency also funded time-sharing research at Berkeley and SDC [System Development Corporation] and supported the installation of time-sharing systems at fourteen other institutions. Now ARPA's total spending on time-sharing runs to $12 million to $13 million a year. At Berkeley the department of electrical engineering and computer science had been suffocating on a yearly budget of $8,000 to $10,000 for computer equipment; ARPA raised the figure to $600,000, which will now be doubled.

While research and support for time-sharing itself went forward, there were, of course, huge advances in general computer technology. Without them, it would have been pointless to talk of time-sharing. In the 1950s there were actually some primitive time-sharing systems, which helped develop the software and hardware of time-sharing. SAGE [semi-automatic ground environment], which feeds the results of many radar observations into central computers and converts the data into displays of identified and unidentified planes in the air, was the first system with some of the elements of time-sharing. Later IBM helped American Airlines establish the SABRE [semi-automatic business reservation environment] reservation system. Thirteen hundred American Airlines agents receive quick answers to as many as two thousand reservation queries a minute from a central processor at Briarcliff Manor, New York. Academics say that these and later airline and hotel reservation systems fall outside the definitions of time-sharing because they are not interactive and can perform only prearranged functions.

Increases in the sheer power of computers are also relevant to time-sharing. It demands big computers. From the vacuum-tube computers of the early 1950s to the integrated-circuit computers of the 1960s, computing power has increased by a factor of about 1,000. The improvement of memories—the libraries of computers—is also important. Time-sharing systems need large memories to store the users' data and programs, and their own operating programs and languages. Not only must the storage be capacious, but retrieval must be rapid. Access time to storage devices such as magnetic drums and disks ranges between 15 and 150 milliseconds. Since 1958, storage costs per character have fallen by a factor of more than twenty while storage capacities have grown as much as a hundredfold.

New kinds of software are even more important in making time-sharing feasible than the new hardware. Computer languages, especially, are vital. The computer itself understands only machine language, that is, electric impulses coded in the binary system to give it data or instructions. [See "The Binary Code," in Section II, below.] It takes an expert to handle machine language and in any case it is slow. The new languages are processed into the computer to translate the dialogue between man and machine. A single English word or phrase can signify a whole series of instructions to the computer, and can also be understood easily by the profane user. Since the first successful language, FORTRAN, was developed at IBM ten years ago, scores of others have proliferated with odd-sounding names made of forced acronyms.

Some of the languages are even forgiving of errors and helpful to inexpert users. Bolt, Beranek & Newman has these elements built into a student-computer dialogue developed for medical students to use in diagnosing illnesses. If the student types poorly and asks the computer for the patient's "plse," the computer says, "Do you mean pulse?" If the student is hasty, the computer sets him straight with phrases such as, "It is common practice in the medical profession to begin an examination by checking the patient's general appearance."

In addition to languages, there are new input-output devices, notably graphic display systems. These are cathode-ray tubes, which can display tables, drawings, and animated flow charts with extraordinary versatility and also receive instructions from a light pen [a light-sensitive pointer] writing on their surfaces. Although they are still far too expensive for general use, some experts think they will become the best tool of any for time-sharing.

## EXPLODING USES [5]

I have no doubt that the fantastic abilities of computers have made automation feasible in many fields, and this is bound to shake up our workaday world dramatically. Dr. Jerome Wiesner, President Kennedy's science adviser and now dean of science at Massachusetts Institute of Technology, considers the development of the computer one of the turning points in history. He predicts:

The computer, with its promise of a millionfold increase in man's capacity to handle information, will undoubtedly have the most far-reaching social consequences of any contemporary technical development.

### Computers Have Variety of Uses

In recent months I have been collecting, with the help of a very diligent secretary, references to new uses of the com-

[5] From pamphlet "Working With Automation," by Sam Zagoria, member of National Labor Relations Board. Condensed transcript from proceedings of the Seminar on Manpower Policy and Program, 1966. United States. Department of Labor. Manpower Administration. Washington, D.C. 20210. '67. p 4-8.

puter. The interesting thing is that hardly a day goes by without a new acquisition. It would take hours to share these with you, so let me select a few as illustrative:

Take transportation, for example. This summer a Pan American jet was landed at Dulles Airport by a computer-operated automatic system, and the crew did nothing but watch and marvel. The computer at the Pennsylvania Railroad can put its finger on each one of 1.8 million freight cars and tell at a glance where it is, whether it is full, empty, or in-between. In Toronto, a computerized traffic control system has speeded the flow of autos by an average of 15 per cent and in some stretches has chopped running time by 34 per cent and reduced accidents at the same time. Outside Pittsburgh, Westinghouse is testing a lightweight, rubber-tired, computer-controlled monorail system which provides service every 2 minutes, in single cars when business is light and longer trains in rush hours. Travel at sea is safeguarded by a string of computer-operated Coast Guard lighthouses that detect fog, switch a foghorn on and off, maintain a radio beacon for navigators, and can even change burned-out lamps if necessary. A recent headline tells the story about a loftier form of transportation: "Computer Lands Gemini Automatically—Commands Are Fed to Thrusters."

The computer has been hooked onto industry, too. It already has a firm place in banks, hotels, airlines, placement agencies, and credit agencies and in the processes of scientific research, typesetting, bookkeeping, listmaking, and income tax checking. But now we are seeing the development of newer uses, such as a computerized asphalt plant which offers precise weight and mix and fast service.

The world's second tallest building is going up in Chicago, with its one hundred stories bearing the imprint of computer designs. The computer enabled the engineers to solve complicated stress analyses that couldn't have been attempted otherwise, saved time, and cut costs. At the nation's largest hydroelectric power facility at Grand Coulee, Washington, computers will monitor 420 relay and circuit breaker contacts one thousand times every second and scan the two hundred bearing temperatures and oil pressures of thirty generators and pumps every fifteen seconds. How's that for surveillance? Even the unions representing plantworkers have hired computers to correlate details of numerous and complicated contracts so that the information on individual provisions is readily available for union negotiators. Data on what other companies are doing adds ammunition to pleas for improvements.

The professions are opening their office doors to the computer, too. Take the medical field, for example. A computer in Washington is analyzing heart conditions of New England patients via long-distance transmission of cardiograms. The time: fifteen seconds. Distance is no obstacle. One cardiogram was taken on an ocean liner in the Atlantic and transmitted by satellite to a specialist in France. At Monmouth Medical Center in New Jersey, the computer maintains patient records, coordinates use of facilities, handles billing and drug orders, and can select healthy, yet economical meals for patients. The Kaiser Foundation Health Plan has harnessed a computer to provide comprehensive physical checkups for three hundred people a day.

In the legal field, more than 3 million Federal and state court decisions have been pumped into a New York City computer and can be searched through by lawyers in seconds. Indeed, the lawyers needn't go to New York, but can make use of the computer via Western Union. Or take education. The computer is entering both the first grade and the graduate school in California. In East Palo Alto, 170 first graders are learning the three Rs from Miss Computer, and at Stanford some three thousand students and faculty members are using computers for their work and studies.

And one last category, matchmaking, the heart of computer activity. In Los Angeles and New York, romantic adult singles are brought together through their common interests as recorded by the computer. At college campuses, computerized dates are described thusly, "We're not taking the love out of love, we're making it more efficient." One test, though, raised some doubts. A computer arranged blind dates for seventy-six married couples based on each person's idea of a perfect date. The result: Only two husbands were matched with their wives.

It is fun admiring American ingenuity in converting a machine to so many uses. It sort of reminds me of the New Jersey boardwalk hucksters I used to enjoy who demonstrated kitchen gadgets that could shred cabbage, split carrots, sculpture radishes, and then convert into combination ladies' hair curlers and men's soldering irons. There is one big difference: These computers really work.

As evidence, take the field of Government. President Johnson, in a memorandum last summer to all departments and agencies, pointed out that the Government's 2,600 computers are making it possible to send men and satellites into space; to make significant strides in medical research; to administer complex income tax, social security, and medicare programs; to manage a multibillion-dollar defense logistics system; and to provide other important services. He directed "every agency head to give thorough study to new ways in which the electronic computer might be used to provide better service to the public, improve agency performance and reduce costs." Private industry, I know, is pursuing a similar course.

### Computer Potential Is Immense

The potential growth of computer usage is immense. As we sit here, the computer industry is growing at a rate faster than any other industry. Around 34,000 computers are now installed in the United States, and the order backlog is more than 23,000. This year [1967] has been described by computer makers as "a great year, a spectacular year, an astounding year," and the future is even brighter. A new development known as molecular electronics is expected to make possible a unit the size of a pinhead, fitting into a computer the size of a carton of cigarettes, and the unit will have no moving parts, heat, or friction. Already, over the past decade, the computer has become 10 times smaller, 100 times faster, and 1,000 times cheaper to operate.

One telling indication of this was given by a businessman who told me that, in deciding where to locate a plant, his company is now more interested in the cost of power than in the cost of labor. This is understandable when you realize that the country's second largest oil refinery, a highly automated one, consumes as much electricity as a city the size of San Antonio, Texas.

What does all this mean to the working men and women of today? Secretary of Labor W. Willard Wirtz said it well a few months after becoming head of the Department of Labor [in 1962]. He said:

Scientific discovery and invention are multiplying man's individual productive power so rapidly that his own place in the scheme of things is being cast in new doubt. A job used to be something that a man expected to have all of his life. And our trouble today is that that is what he still expects. But it is no longer true. In an age of technology triumphant, of exploding population, a man's job is the product of unpredictable but almost certain change.

Already this year's school graduates have been warned that they may expect, on the average, to move into six or seven jobs during their forty-three-year work-life in our mobile economy. This is the result of change, and compression, since education is becoming longer and retirement earlier.

The acceleration in the tempo of change comes about because the timelag between discovery and commercial application has been shortened; the timelag between development and widespread adoption has narrowed. Think of the giant steps the television industry has made in less than twenty years and how many millions of us took each step. It has gone from tiny receivers to huge black and white or color sets, to portable or theatre screen sets, to constantly lighter, transistorized units, to intercontinental satellite transmission, and now deluxe three-course TV dinners. Our nine-year-old wonders how we ever got along without television. Indeed, how did we?

## THE MAN-MACHINE PARTNERSHIP [6]

The history of machines, from the wheel to the spaceship, reflects man's progress in controlling nature and in supplementing and extending his own human capabilities.

First he extended his physical capabilities, his muscle power, to plow his fields, transport himself and his goods, and industrialize his society.

Then he extended his sensory powers—his vision, touch, and hearing—to observe nature better, make measurements, and communicate over large distances.

Today, in a third broad stride, man is developing machines to supplement and extend his cognitive powers, his abilities to think and reason and learn.

Although this third era has only begun to show itself, already it commands our attention. Demonstrations of technical advances already made impel us to expect this age of cognitive machines to move from infancy to maturity in decades rather than centuries or millennia as did the other machine eras.

The new machines—call them computers for now—can store and retrieve information in huge amounts, analyze and synthesize data, perform logic, and communicate with humans in ordinary human languages.

### Elbow to Elbow

Because it can do these things, a machine of this kind can serve man as a close partner, helping him while he works in creative, intellectual pursuits. This partnership, as it evolves, will expand the range of tasks man can undertake and will enable him to solve problems that are much too complex for him to solve alone.

[6] From "Machines Are 'Talking Back,'" by Dr. Richard H. Bolt, chairman of Bolt, Beranek & Newman, Inc. *Christian Science Monitor.* p 9. Jl. 20, '67. Reprinted by permission from *The Christian Science Monitor.* © 1967 The Christian Science Publishing Society. All rights reserved.

At the very outset we face a difficulty in talking about this new way of working with machines: Neither its name nor its scope has been defined in any generally accepted terms. Science and technology often force us to redefine familiar words. Some of the words we now must reconsider are *partner, intellectual, computer, think, communicate, reason.*

Webster's unabridged *New International Dictionary* gives as one of several definitions of the verb *to reason:* ". . . to attempt to arrive at a conclusion through induction, deduction, or a combination of these; as, man alone reasons. . . ."

## New Terms Needed

Names that have been used to designate the man-machine relationship we are discussing include *computer time-sharing, man-computer symbiosis, on-line problem solving, synnoesis,* and many other words and phrases. Without implying that our terms are preferred ones, we shall use *the partnership* to designate the man and the machine working together, and *machine-aided cognition* to mean the process by which they jointly work in intellectual endeavor.

Because the machine, as well as the man, possesses the faculties of memory and association, we can indeed say that the man and the machine are thinking as a team. An updated paraphrase of Webster in the future might read, ". . . man *not* alone reasons. . . ."

An even more basic semantic difficulty stems from the word *computer,* which would seem to mean a machine that just computes. A better choice might have been *symbolater:* a machine that manipulates symbols in accordance with logical rules.

The symbols it can manipulate are not only the numerals and mathematical symbols used in computing, but also the letters of the alphabet, the words and sentences of language, notes representing musical sounds, graphic drawings, and in fact abstract symbols of any kind.

Further, the machine can select, arrange, and relate symbols in any manner whatever, not only in the manner of mathematical computation. More precisely, we should say that the machine can be programmed or taught to do any of these things.

The progress of civilization reflects the extent to which man utilizes abstract symbols to represent things and events and ideas. In the modern world, unless a worker is engaged in manipulating physical materials and objects, he is engaged almost totally in manipulating symbols. Therefore the new machines, whether we call them computers or symbolaters, have shown up as timely inventions mothered by necessity.

When they were first developed, however, computers were used mainly for computing, in the strict sense of the word. Today, when they are adapted for use in machine-aided cognition, computers are being used in ways that were not expected when they were first designed. In the future, the nonhuman part of the partnership may bear little resemblance to the computers we know today.

Computers, then, were designed to calculate mathematical relations among numbers and perform logical operations using symbols.

## Communication Expander

In order to serve as a useful partner in cognition, the machine must be able to communicate not only in numbers but also in the verbal forms of language and in graphical abstractions. What is more, the machine must be able to carry out not only simple mathematical rules, but also logical operations more complex than any that today's computers normally handle.

We are making two distinctions, one about language and one about complexity. Advancing from numerical to verbal and graphical language is not an easy step, but the reward is simply the one we gain from learning a foreign language: Now we can communicate where before we could not. Once we have achieved linguistic communication with the machine, however, we then can develop an ever-expanding ability to work together in complex processes of thought, and we can apply this ability to all spheres of intellectual endeavor.

How can a machine communicate with humans? The first requirement is the ability to take in and give out information in ways that both partners can handle. Especially, the modes of communication must be easy and natural for the human to use so that the mechanics of giving and getting information will not impede the flow of thoughts and insights.

### Input Equals Ears

When two persons communicate, each can send information, as by talking, writing, drawing, or typing. And each can receive information, mainly through hearing and seeing. The mechanisms we humans use for communicating are mainly the voice, hands, ears, and eyes.

The machine counterparts go by the names input and output devices. They include microphones and loudspeakers, knobs and push buttons, electrically operated typewriters, display screens, writing tablets, and penlike instruments with which a man can write on a screen or tablet in such a way that the machine can see what he writes.

Today we communicate with a machine partner mostly through electric typewriters and teletypewriters. For example, using a particular computation service that now is provided commercially, like telephone service, we can type the instruction, "TYPE 2+2" and the teletypewriter—operated by a computer that may be many miles away—automatically types back "2+2 equals 4." Of course the machine has learned to do much more than first-grade arithmetic.

This service is helping scientists and engineers solve complex computational problems, such as those met in designing space systems, chemical plants, and highways.

Another example of communication by typing is a machine that has been programmed to get information by asking you to fill out a questionnaire. The machine might type as its first question, "1.1 NAME" and you might respond, "JONES, JOHN J." meaning the name of a pupil you are enrolling in school.

This machine we usually call a system—an information-communication system. It comprises not only a central computer and computer programs of many kinds, but also a network of communication lines and input-output devices connected to the ends of the lines.

## Books via TV

When it communicates through a typewriter, the machine usually types faster and more accurately than the human user. However, typing is a skill in which humans can become very adept, and judging by the enthusiasm of many elementary pupils who have participated in computer experiments during the past three years, we can expect that learning to type will someday become as common as learning the three Rs.

A quite different input-output device is the cathode-ray screen, such as the face of a television set, which can display textual and graphical material as well as pictures, both moving and still. A display screen can show a paragraph or even an entire page of text from a book that the human user is reading. The user, in turn, can put a message into the screen by using a light pen, a light-sensitive pointer with which he touches the screen or writes on it.

The display screen and light pen have been used, for example, in a system devised to help persons study and edit documents. Using an electric typewriter to give auxiliary commands, the user asks for certain pages of text, which he may first wish to scan rapidly. The pages can come from any number of books and articles that have been stored in the memory of the system (such as a tape on which magnetic patterns have been induced).

## Editing Possible

When the user sees a sentence or paragraph of interest, he touches that part of the text with his light pen and asks the system to hold it for future reference. He can also, again using the light pen, write marginal notes on the screen. These might be short descriptors or labels that classify the material as to different topics or ideas he is studying.

After he has thus examined all the documents he wants to, the user asks the system to display just those pieces of text that he has designated, and to reassemble them according to the topics indicated, in a specified order. Then, still using his light pen, he crosses out superfluous words, rearranges sentences, and in other ways edits the selected passages at will. Perhaps he is preparing a technical abstract or a legal brief, and later he will ask the system to type a clean copy of his edited text.

In some professions, such as architecture, city planning, industrial design, and animated filmmaking, man often creates ideas and solves problems more naturally through drawings than through words.

Machines now can draw, read, and interpret graphical information, communicating through devices such as the display screen and light pen, the graphical input tablet and stylus, and the automatic graphical plotter.

Machines also can create drawings in accordance with logical principles and design goals put in by the man. In making an animated film, for example, the artist can draw a basic human figure and specify possible motions of the limbs and body, and the machine then can draw many frames showing the figure turning and walking away.

Another system is helping highway engineers analyze contour maps, calculate earth-removal requirements and costs, draw the grading and landscaping, and produce a movie that lets you see from the driver's seat what it would be like to drive along the proposed highway.

### Step-by-Step Flexibility

Above all, machine-aided cognition will help man to deal with complexity, to solve complex problems. By this we mean problems that cannot be solved all at once through a complete set of procedures specified in advance, but only through a step-by-step approach in which a discovery made at one step will suggest what step should come next.

Computers conventionally perform batch-processing, that is a well-defined job, in accordance with a complete, errorless set of rules, a computer program, which is specified fully in advance. Machine-aided cognition replaces batch-processing with a more flexible partnership between man and machine. Together they travel along an uncharted path, making a sequence of decisions among unforeseen alternatives, as they work their way toward a solution of the complex problem.

Although this newest machine age is scarcely one decade old, the potential it offers for supplementing human capabilities is clearly visible, at least in the research laboratories. Adding its logical power in dealing with symbols to the imaginative insight of the human, the machine will make possible a level of creative intellectual achievement that in the past could be attained only through a long and grueling process of trial and error—if at all.

## THE SOCIAL IMPACT [7]

Automation as an engineering phenomenon may be discussed more or less objectively, but when we consider the impact of automation on society, vested interests, personal values, beliefs and uninformed opinion enter the picture. Automation is part of the larger process of social change which has been going on in human society since its inception.

In the long run of history, man has evolved various technologies through which he has satisfied his needs and wants. The first involved either manual manipulation of the environment or the use of crude tools. At a later stage tools were combined to produce machines. Now we stand at a

[7] From "The Impact of Automation on Society," by Frederick L. Bates, chairman of the Department of Sociology and Anthropology at the University of Georgia. *Bulletin of the Atomic Scientists.* 25:4-6. Je. '69. Reprinted by permission.

stage in the process of technological development when machines have become self-operating.

It is important to realize that within the total technology of society all of the forms of implements that have evolved throughout man's history are still in use. Most of the behavior of human beings in pursuit of goals or in the production of desired goods is still in the premachine stage of technological development. In most of the world, family life, religion, education, agriculture, government and recreation, and, for the most part, production of goods and services, are carried on with a premechanized or premachine technology. In viewing man from a world perspective, we must recognize, therefore, that there exist side by side the most primitive and the most sophisticated technological schemes.

Since automation represents the highest development of technology, it is inevitable that industry will move in its direction. While there are strong values that act as motivating forces toward automation, there exist simultaneously other values that work against it. American society places value on full employment of the labor force. Americans hold that an adult male who is not physically or mentally disabled should work for a living and contribute to the productive system. Americans believe that a man's moral fiber and character are developed through work and destroyed by indolence and leisure, that if a person receives income without a just claim upon it through his labor he will be demoralized by the process. Still another belief is that machines and computers dehumanize life and threaten to make slaves of men. On these values rests the great concern over the long-run effects of automation.

## Right to Consume

Our social order is founded on the proposition that a man's right to consume the products of technology is established through the role he performs in the productive process. The more important the role, the greater is the share to which he is entitled in the consumption of the outpourings of the technological system. Carried to its extreme this proposition leads to the conclusion that a person who performs no role in production has no right to consume. Other values within our society, however, mitigate the harshness of this formula. They lead to programs of public welfare which provide at least minimum subsistence for persons who have no "legitimate" role in production.

In the approach to the poverty problem in our society, there is a dominant theme which states that the role in production measures the right to consume. Our society is attempting to eliminate poverty by creating full employment. By so doing, we try to establish a person's claim to consume the fruits of the economic system without altering either our values or our social organization. Thus, public policy is aimed at achieving full employment through the creation of new jobs and new economic opportunities.

### The "Technophobiacs"

There are some counterproposals that disturb the man on the street. The rise of groups within society which have a different perspective toward the economic and social order is a fact of our times. They challenge the basic tenets of society. The major sources of these dissonant notes in the buzzing harmony of our industrialized social order come from the youth who have not yet entered the labor force; from the poor, especially the black poor, who have been locked out of it; and from intellectuals who, by the nature of their roles, are detached from it. It is not surprising that the largest number of "technophobiacs" are found among the ranks of the poor, the young and the professional thinkers.

A strong case can be made for saying that the present, rebellious generation of college students represents the first class of individuals who have experienced, for a lifetime, the new affluence and leisure created by the technological developments of the last century. Prior to this generation, most youths experienced work as a part of life and also deprivation, at least in a mild form, as part of their membership in society. The present generation of college students knows it is possible to consume without being actively employed in the production process. Their consumption for a lifetime has been based on a "right" rather than a "role." At the same time, they are acutely aware of the fact that they live in a society with people who do not share in the level of consumption the present college generation takes for granted. This leads disaffected youth to challenge the basic values of society and, at the same time, its organization.

## New Left and Civil Rights

They propose new values on the assumption that society is a flexible instrument for attaining human ends and may be changed to suit new purposes without destroying old levels of production and consumption. The youthful New Left seems, therefore, to be a result of certain technological developments which have created a new condition for youth in society, and which have led to a new way of looking at the relationship between roles in the production process and the right to consume.

The civil rights movement is also intimately intertwined with technological development. A large segment of the population is seeking a new and more satisfying role in the world of work at a time when such roles are rapidly disappearing. These roles are disappearing not as a result of the infant automation process but as a result of mechanization. Curiously enough, mechanization (which has most recently displaced human labor) has occurred mainly in agriculture rather than industry. It has caused major shifts in the ecological pattern of farming and has produced mass migrations and social mobility. Millions of black sharecroppers and tenant farmers and their families, along with millions of white marginal land owners and tenants, have been forced off the land and into cities and towns. They have arrived there without industrial skills, seeking employment that will give them the right to consume, or perhaps just to subsist. This set of circumstances has been the major force behind

the civil rights movement. It cannot be attributed to automation, or even to industry. It is an agricultural development.

## A Suspicious Triangle

It is hardly debatable that the youth movement and the
civil rights movement will have considerable impact on the
future rate of mechanization in industry, and certainly on
the rate at which future automation occurs. The New Left
which represents an alliance between middle and upper class
youth, black people and the intelligentsia, forming an uneasy and mutually suspicious triangle, is trying to define a
new set of values. These are based on a combination of myth
and fact about the nature of society and the nature of technology. Part of the mythology arises from the belief that,
given the right way of organizing things, we are capable of
producing sufficient goods and services to satisfy all significant and legitimate human needs in the foreseeable future.
Yet there exists within the belief system a suspicion and distrust of machines and machine systems as being the major
dehumanizing agents in society.

Another part of the mythology relates to the notion of
power structure and the functioning of the decision-making
processes of society. Here the power structure is visualized
as if it were a gigantic machine grinding out decisions in a
conspiracy to enslave human beings by tying them to a technological process which becomes an end in itself. No matter
whether these beliefs correspond in any way to fact, they
may foreshadow a new time of troubles in the so-called industrial revolution, a time of slowing down, rather than
advancement.

## State of Ignorance

Those who believe that revolutionary or cataclysmic social changes, produced by deliberately induced anarchy,
could enhance technological development make claims to
understanding the intricacies of advanced societies that are
totally unsupported by the state of knowledge of how soci-

eties operate. Even if the wisest and most humanitarian group of persons on earth was assembled to redesign our society along Utopian lines, it would have to act largely on the basis of beliefs, values, prejudices and preferences rather than on scientifically reliable knowledge. Out of such a planning process, given our current state of ignorance of the principles of social organization, would come more errors, causing greater human deprivation and suffering than would occur by a less deliberate process of social adaptation.

It is because we are so ignorant of the inner workings of social systems that we are in this predicament. We know more about building rockets and computers, or automating production processes, than we do about constructing human social systems to meet human needs. We can set out to send men to the moon with reasonable assurance that we will succeed. Yet we are so ignorant about the functioning of society that we cannot set out to eliminate poverty, crime or air pollution, or to promote rapid, undamaging technological development with a reasonable assurance of success.

It is our ignorance of the inner workings of society that forces us to choose between unguided, automatic, gradual, adaptive change on the one hand or dogma-guided, deliberately controlled change on the other. Going on the basis of some all-or-nothing revolutionary plan is like Icarus setting out for the sun on wings of feathers and beeswax. Going on the basis of automatic, uncontrolled change is like putting up the family plantation as a stake in a crap game where the dice are loaded against us. In our state of ignorance, we are forced either to gamble on the age-old, laissez-faire adaptive processes, or on following some new, charismatic, social philosopher whose knowledge of the nature and functioning of human society is faulty at best.

Given the state of our present social science knowledge, the best we can do is to forecast probable developments and anticipate some of the problems that seem likely to accompany them. This should lead us to attempt to develop scientific knowledge of these trends so that we may establish mastery over our own society as well as over the natural environment.

There are several directions our society is likely to take in adapting to mechanization and automation. Instead of allowing unemployment to grow, our society is much more likely to move in the direction of shrinking the amount of work done by the average worker. This may occur by increasing the age of entrance into the work force, shortening the workday or workweek, lowering the age of retirement and increasing vacations.

## Psychedelic Trend

Other patterns in society must be elaborated in order to take up the slack time left over by such a solution. Nonwork activities may be indicated by the directions that societies have taken in the past when they reached a juncture similar to one we have reached. In the future, a much greater amount of time will be spent by the average individual on narcissistic activities, such as personal grooming, dress, bathing, plastic surgery and dentistry, physical culture and health. Related to the narcissistic trend is one toward emphasizing the senses as a source of pleasure. The development of psychedelic drugs and their surrounding patterns of art and music, as well as the orgiastic organization of numbers of hippie communities, point inevitably to the development of the sensate.

Continued technological development will result in certain structural changes in society. The size of future economic enterprises will far exceed their present scale, and will be measured in terms of their output rather than in numbers of employees. This trend can be seen today in the petrochemical industry where automation is more nearly complete than in other sectors of industry. Growth in the scale of government can be expected to parallel growth in organizations in the private sector.

One direction our society could go is toward an increase in activities which provide a continuous escape valve for our excess of productivity over domestic, nonmilitary consumption.

## Space Exploration

The explorations of inner and outer space provide particularly fertile fields for accomplishing such a purpose. For one thing, space hardware is fabricated by the opposite kinds of productive process from automation. It is virtually handmade. Because of the necessity for great precision and reliability, it requires fantastic amounts of human labor in testing and inspection.

Furthermore, even though spacecraft and their launching, monitoring and recovery systems are largely automated, they require large crews of highly trained and paid experts to design and operate them. They present an example of how automation and technological development have created a whole system of new occupations and jobs. These in themselves do not produce consumable goods but they create purchasing power for the goods. It is anticipated that a similar movement to explore the seas will one day be undertaken by our society. Such a program will parallel the present one in aerospace in its economic functions.

We are moving toward a supernational economic and political structure. It seems improbable, therefore, that foreign aid and foreign investment of private capital will decrease significantly. However, increased productive capacity in other nations, as well as our own, and the trend toward automation will transpose our own dilemma over the use of our industrial plant for human needs to the level of an international problem.

# II. WHAT MANNER OF MACHINE IS THIS?

## EDITOR'S INTRODUCTION

So quickly has the computer taken hold in our society that it has spawned a peculiar kind of folklore of its own. In almost any newspaper or magazine one can find a story of some fantastic new use the computer has been put to—be it matching up possible marriage partners or figuring out the opposing team's football strategy. One result of such stories is the widespread impression that computers are capable of anything and everything.

In fact, of course, a computer is a very specific entity, operating in a relatively simple way, capable of solving only those problems that have been properly prepared for it by human minds. What it does and how it does it is the subject of this section.

The first selection addresses itself to what may seem to be a deceptively simple question—just what is a computer and what makes it so significant? The answer, we find, is that basically a computer is a very fast and accurate calculator working with a simple kind of mathematics. The next article in the section explains how this kind of mathematics is used and how it differs from the decimal system we use daily.

Does that mean we just learn the new math and push numbers into a computer? It could be done that way. But it would be much too cumbersome and time-consuming to use in solving a simple problem. To shortcut the process men have developed highly sophisticated ways of preparing problems—or programming them—for computer use. The third article tells how this is done.

The article that follows examines in detail what happens to a problem once it gets into the computer, and how it is solved. The payroll problem the article describes is a typical business application of the computer, but the same principles can be used to solve problems in other fields. The selection that follows is a series of thumbnail sketches of how computers are used in a variety of fields.

So far in this section we have dealt with digital computers because they are far and away the most common kind in use. But the digital computer as a "little brother," the analog computer. What it does and how it does it is the subject of the last article in the section.

## WHAT IS A COMPUTER? [1]

In the few short years since it was developed, the computer has profoundly affected all of us. Every day we hear of new ways in which the computer has changed ways of doing things. It helps to predict our elections, guide our astronauts in space, control our traffic, forecast the weather, compute our bank statements, and does hundreds of other tasks that were unheard of a generation ago.

It's not at all hard to think of the computer as an electronic wizard. But it isn't magical. Like the television set in your living room, the computer is simply a piece of electronic equipment. Unlike your television set, which is designed to entertain you, the computer is designed to solve problems.

Why, then, do we hear so much about the computer? What makes it a better problem-solver than, say, a hardy Ph.D. with an adding machine? Just what does a computer do, and how does it do it?

We are familiar with everyday devices like the washing machine, the telephone, the stoplight on the corner. We use them and we work with them, although we may not know exactly how they work. But many of us don't know what computers are, because comparatively few of us see them, use them or work with them.

[1] From pamphlet, "Introducing . . . the Computer," by Fred C. Gielow, Jr., senior associate engineer in IBM's Systems Development Division. International Business Machines Corporation. Data Processing Division. 112 E. Post Rd. White Plains, N.Y. 10601. (no date) p 3-10. Reprinted by permission.

It may surprise you, but the washing machine, the telephone, and the stoplight on the corner are computers in their own right. They have the same basic elements of operation: input, processing and output.

For the washing machine, the input is dirty clothes (and soap or detergent), the processing is their washing, and the output is the same clothes—clean.

For the telephone, input is the telephone number, processing is the decoding of that number to open and close switches, and output is the completed connection to the person you dialed.

For the stoplight on the corner, input is a coded timing mechanism, processing is its activation, and output is the continuous cycling of lights: red, green, amber, red, green, amber. . . .

For the computer, input consists of a program and data. Processing is when the computer uses the program to operate on the data—to solve an equation, for example. Output is the solution—to the equation, or to whatever problem was programmed.

Are your ideas of what a computer is still a little unclear? Let's take a spin in a washing machine and explore the similarities between a washer and a computer.

### Cycles, or "Programs"

Your washing machine, like many others, may have several cycles from which to choose. You can wash dainty, delicate items in a gentle cold-water cycle. You can wash shirts in a stronger warm-water cycle, and you can get filthy flannels sparkling clean in a heavy-duty hot-water cycle. There may be as many as six or eight cycles to choose from.

These cycles are no more than the "programs" of your washing machine. Cycle One—call it Program One—gives you cold water, easy washing action, three rinses, no deep rinse, and a spin. Program Two gives you warm water, hard washing action, three rinses, a deep rinse, and a long spin. And so on.

When you wash your clothes you simply specify the program you want . . . by turning a knob or pushing a button.

Let's say you have a computer with eight programs. Program One will add a number three times, multiply it twice, and subtract it twice. Program Two will add a number six times, multiply it three times, subtract it four times, and divide it once.

When you have some numbers you wish to add, subtract, multiply or divide, you simply specify the program you want. You might put the numbers into your computer from a special typewriter, and designate the program you want by turning a knob or pushing a button.

While having eight programs for your washing machine may be ample, only eight programs for your computer are far too few. How many problems can you solve with a program that only adds three times, multiplies twice and subtracts twice?

What would happen if we allowed our programs more flexibility? Let's design your washing machine so that you can choose the water temperature separately, the number of rinses, the precise way any action will occur, and moreover, choose the sequence in which the actions will occur. You might instruct your washing machine to rinse 101 times, or you could start your washing program with three long spins.

This flexibility would allow you to instruct the machine to do precisely what you wanted . . . to get your clothes clean.

And so it is with your computer. You, the computer programmer, can instruct your machine to add, subtract, multiply, divide, and do dozens of other actions in any sequence you wish, to solve any problems you wish. A combination of these instructions forms a program, and the program will do precisely what you want it to do (assuming you make no mistakes).

### Four Reasons for Greatness

But you can use an adding machine or calculator to add, subtract, multiply and divide. Why, then, is the computer so great? There are four major reasons.

First is speed. The computer is so fast that it saves a tremendous amount of time. A computer's lightning speed
makes it possible, for the first time, to tackle problems that
are so large as to make them impossible the pencil-and-paper
way (or for that matter, the Ph.D.-and-adding-machine way).

For example, let's say it takes you ten seconds to add two
four-digit numbers together. In that time, a medium-size
computer can add a million four-digit numbers together. Or,
to put it another way, to do all the adding a computer can
do in ten seconds would take you more than one hundred
days, and that's allowing no time for sleeping, eating or
pencil sharpening.

The second reason for the computer's greatness is its accuracy. You know how hard it is to balance your checking
account. Just imagine balancing 10,000 checking accounts
(in only ten seconds) without one mistake—not even one
penny in error. That's what the computer can do, and it
performs with unerring accuracy second after second, hour
after hour.

The third reason for the computer's greatness is the discipline it imposes. To solve a problem with a computer you
must, first, understand the problem, and, second, program
the computer to give you the right answer. Understanding a
problem is one thing, but understanding it to the depth of
detail and insight required to program the computer is a
completely different matter.

By setting a dial on your washing machine to Heavy
Duty Cycle you can get a wide variety of laundry clean. However, you could get any one type of laundry cleaner if you
could specify exact water temperatures, exact length of wash
cycle, speed of agitator, and so on. But you would have to
know much more about the laundry—and its condition—to
take advantage of the full potential of the washing machine's
great flexibility.

To program a computer to help teach children about
economics, you must know a great deal about economics.
You have to know a great deal about the learning process,

too. To program a computer to keep track of all the stock in your warehouse, you must know a lot about inventory control and operations research techniques and you have to know the answers to basic policy questions about your company. The discipline, the understanding, the insight: these benefits are the indirect results of solving a problem with a computer.

### Arithmetic Plus

The fourth reason for the computer's greatness is its versatility. A computer can do much more than just add, subtract, multiply and divide. It's a little like a washing machine that can wash the clothes, sort them out, iron them, and put them away for you, too. Similarly, a computer, by using instructions, can sort data, straighten data out and store it away for you.

Instructions allow the computer to compare two numbers, to find out if one is larger than, smaller than, or equal to the other. By comparing, it can sort. It can arrange a list of numbers in a given order into another list in any other order. It does this with a sort program.

A computer also uses "branching" instructions. These are used to jump around in a program. Think of a program as a list of orders (that's exactly what a program is). Suppose after order number ten, you, as programmer, want to jump, for some reason, to order number fifteen. You specify this with a branch (it's sometimes called transfer) instruction.

Another family of computer instructions is used for input-output operations. How efficient your washing machine would be if you could write a program for it like this:

Are clothes clean?

If not, *branch* to Rewash Program
If so, continue

Are clothes dry?

If not, *branch* to Drying Program
If so, continue

Are clothes ironed?

If so, *branch* to Put-Away Program (see below)

If not, should clothes be ironed?

If so, *branch* to Iron Program

If not, *branch* to Put-Away Program

*Put-Away Program*

Put pillowcases in the linen closet

Put handkerchiefs in bureau drawer (top, left)

Put flannels in bureau drawer (bottom, center)

Put shirts in closet (to the right of the pants)

Put crib sheets in baby's room

Put Grandma Nelly's old crazy quilt in the attic

Put the green towels in the blue bathroom

Put the blue towels in the green bathroom

Put any stones, marbles, string, etc., from children's pants
    in the trash

The "put" instructions for the washing machine are the output instructions for the computer. Any data in the computer can be printed on a form, punched in cards, written on magnetic tape, shown on a TV-like display, or sent out of the computer in any of several other forms.

Just as there are output instructions, there are input instructions. It's like having the washing machine round up the dirty clothes for a wash.

Punched cards and magnetic tape are popular means of storage for data kept outside the computer. But the computer also needs storage space inside to work with. For a program to run, it must be inside the computer. When the computer works with data, the data must be inside the computer.

This internal storage is usually called the computer memory. Data is read into the memory from punched cards or magnetic tape (or another external storage device), processed, and then written out on cards or tape (or some other medium). And this is the computer cycle: input, processing, output. Put in the dirty clothes, agitate them a bit, and get clean clothes out.

There are some other points our washing machine analogy can clarify for us. Let's examine several popular, but quite inaccurate, notions about the computer.

### The "Thinking" Machine

First, the computer as a "thinking machine." The computer cannot think, any more than the washing machine can think. What it can do is extend man's problem-solving capabilities by performing many arithmetic, logic, branching and input-output instructions with lightning speed. The computer doesn't really decide election results. It merely presents the results of a carefully written statistical-analysis program that calculates election probabilities. That's why the predictions of one computer don't always agree with those of another. The computers don't disagree. Rather, it's the analysts and statisticians and programmers who wrote the programs for the computers who disagree.

A second area of confusion is the importance of data. Even though you have a flawless program and an excellent computer, you may get nonsense instead of the result you seek. Why? Because of the data. If the data you use is wrong (for example, the number of votes for each candidate from the sample voting areas) you may well get the wrong answer (you may name the wrong candidate as winner).

In the computer world, programmers have a name for it: GIGO (Garbage In, Garbage Out). With our washing machine analogy, it means that even with the right program, if we put garbage in, we won't get clean clothes out. What we get out may be clean, but it will still be garbage.

A third misconception about computers is their so-called failures. We hear about the computer that printed a paycheck for $1.25 million instead of $125.00, the correct amount. We hear of the computer that continued to print increasingly severe delinquent payment notices, despite the fact that the payment had long ago been received and deposited. What about these flagrant mistakes?

Well, chances are it wasn't the fault of the computer, but much more likely a program that hadn't been completely proven, a program with some bugs or errors remaining in it.

That's not to say the computer never fails. After all, like the washing machine, it has parts that can wear out. But, also like the washing machine, it generally lets you know when it fails. It doesn't take you thirty-seven loads of wash to discover that the water isn't coming on in your machine. In a similar way, when a computer has a failure, you can usually spot it quickly.

The programming bug is another kind of animal. If you're writing and debugging a program, you may have tested your work until you'd stake a high wager on its perfection. But programming can be a very humbling experience, and there is a good chance that when your program is used for production runs, you'll get some totally unexpected results. Maybe not the first day or the first week, but sooner or later you're likely to get a surprise: the wrong answer.

The point of all this is that though computers are not infallible, usually it's the man-made program that causes the goofs.

### Don't Blame the Machine!

Another source of confusion about computers is illustrated when a company executive makes a statement like this:

What's wrong with our computers anyway? They give the right answers, but they don't give us the information we want the way we want it.

The computer is a general-purpose problem-solver, and to make this type of statement is like saying you need a new car when you make a wrong turn and get yourself lost. Here again the finger of suspicion can be pointed at the program or at the analysis of what was needed. Perhaps the executive who made the statement and the programmer who wrote the program had not successfully communicated. The desires of one were not reflected in the designs of the other.

The computer is a big, dumb machine, dependent entirely on those who control it. Forget to put soap or detergent in your washer, and you may be disappointed with its results. Use the wrong or a faulty program, or use the wrong or inaccurate data, and you will get the wrong answer.

Although we have compared the computer to the washing machine in many ways, we should remember that the computer is unique. It allows man to solve more problems, more rapidly and more accurately, than ever before. It broadens the pool of problems man can solve. It extends man's learning and understanding. Unlike so many other machines that help man solve problems with his muscles, the computer helps man solve problems with his mind.

## THE BINARY CODE [2]

The computer's language is written in binary code. It is a simple way of communicating, once you get the hang of it. Third and fourth grade children in many parts of the country are learning binary as part of New Math.

If you already understand binary, you know that there are really just two new ideas that must be grasped:

First, whereas decimal numbers—the kind of numbers we ordinarily use—are built on a base of 10, binary numbers are on a base of 2. The base 10 means that when you move a digit one space to the left (and add a zero), it's worth 10 times as much. Another way of saying this is that it increases by the power of 10. With binary numbers, using a base of two, every time you move a number to the left, it's worth 2 times as much, or it increases by the power of 2.

Just as in the decimal system, based on the power of ten, the value increases from right to left, so do values in the

[2] From pamphlet, "You and the Computer: A Student's Guide," General Electric Company. 570 Lexington Ave. New York 10022. '65. p 10. © 1965 by the General Electric Company. Reprinted by permission.

binary system increase from right to left by the value of the base. By way of illustration:

Decimal:    1,000   -   100   -   10   -   1
Binary:     32  -  16  -  8  -  4  -  2  -  1

The second thing to learn about binary is that the system uses only two numbers: 1 and 0. In other words, you must forget about the numbers 2, 3, 4, 5, 6, 7, 8, and 9. They are never used in the binary system.

So the question arises, how do you count to two, without a 2? It's simple. As we noted, the value of the binary number increases by two times as you move it one space to the left. To get two in binary then, you simply move your 1 one space to the left and add zero. Thus, 10 in binary is the same as 2 in decimal.

To visualize this imagine two cars—one has a mileage indicator in the regular decimal system, the other has a mileage indicator in the binary system. At the start of a race, mileage indicators on each car read: 00000. Now watch what happens as they go down the road:

| Binary |  | Decimal |
|--------|-----------------|---------|
| 00000 | start | 00000 |
| 00001 | first mile | 00001 |
| 00010 | second mile | 00002 |
| 00011 | third mile | 00003 |
| 00100 | fourth mile | 00004 |
| 00101 | fifth mile | 00005 |
| 00110 | sixth mile | 00006 |
| 00111 | seventh mile | 00007 |
| 01000 | eighth mile | 00008 |
| 01001 | ninth mile | 00009 |
| 01010 | tenth mile | 00010 |
| 01011 | eleventh mile | 00011 |
| 01100 | twelfth mile | 00012 |
| 01101 | thirteenth mile | 00013 |
| 01110 | fourteenth mile | 00014 |
| 01111 | fifteenth mile | 00015 |

| 10000 | sixteenth mile | 00016 |
| ----- | seventeenth mile | 00017 |
| ----- | eighteenth mile | 00018 |
| ----- | nineteenth mile | 00019 |
| ----- | twentieth mile | 00020 |
| ----- | twenty-first mile | 00021 |
| ----- | twenty-second mile | 00022 |
| ----- | twenty-third mile | 00023 |
| ----- | twenty-fourth mile | 00024 |
| 11001 | twenty-fifth mile | 00025 |

(Fill in the blanks in the binary column.)

There is an easy way to convert a binary number to decimal. Just write down the successive powers of 2, then underneath match up the binary number. Take binary number 1100101:

$$64 \quad 32 \quad 16 \quad 8 \quad 4 \quad 2 \quad 1$$
$$1 \quad 1 \quad 0 \quad 0 \quad 1 \quad 0 \quad 1$$
$$64+32 \quad + \quad 4 + \quad 1=101$$

Each digit—either a 1 or a 0—in a binary number is called a bit (short for binary digit). This is important to remember because, as we will see, information moves through a computer a bit at a time.

While the binary code may seem a bit awkward to those who are used to the decimal system, it is simplicity itself to the computer. This is because the basic electronic parts inside the computer can exist in only two possible states: current is on or off, a switch is open or closed, magnetic materials are magnetized in one direction or the opposite.

## PROGRAMMING: WORDS THAT MOVE MACHINES [3]

Computers have undergone some dramatic changes since they were first introduced commercially some dozen years

[3] Pamphlet. International Business Machines Corporation. Data Processing Division. 112 E. Post Rd. White Plains, N.Y. 10601. (no date) p 3-10. Reprinted by permission.

ago. Most of the fanfare concerning these improvements has centered on equipment—the progress from tube to transistor to present solid logic circuitry. Behind these physical changes, however, lies an equally dramatic and even more important story: the evolutionary changes in the techniques of programming.

The inherent capabilities of a computer are myriad but sometimes difficult to employ. Through programming, the general-purpose computer changes into a machine capable of performing an almost endless variety of special-purpose jobs—one minute updating inventory, the next calculating commissions, solving engineering equations, scheduling shipments or simulating market conditions. In every case, the computer's skill is only a reflection of the ingenuity of the man or men who wrote the instructions.

This ability involves both science and art. The science of programming lies in analyzing a problem and then reducing it to the sequence of small steps the computer can use in solving it. The art, on the other hand, lies in the ability to utilize the basic steps of the machine in an endless variety of ways. Just as we can use the twenty-six letters of the alphabet to produce an almost infinite variety of words, the programmer can combine basic computer operations into a limitless number of programs.

## The Language Barrier

Translating concepts and commands into machine language is the essence of programming. We think and work in the broad and expressive idiom of English; computers respond only to a very narrow and rigid number code. For this reason in the early years of the computer age almost as much work was devoted to translating program instructions into computer code as in devising the steps of a program itself. (An instruction, when translated into the binary form of ones and zeros, causes appropriate electrical paths to close in the computer. In computer terms, this action is called an instruction fetch and decode. Data also enters the computer in the form of binary ones and zeros, and is put into machine-recognizable form. This data manipulation occurs during execute time.)

Breaking down the language barrier is a major goal of programming research. The earliest stored-program computers required the programmer to write instructions directly in the language of the machine—in long lists of numbers. It was not only a time-consuming, tedious and essentially clerical process, but was prone to numerous errors. After analyzing his problem, the programmer had to reduce every piece of it, and every command, down to the basic number code of the machine: sometimes tens of thousands of code words. He also had to assign data to specific storage locations and provide for changing storage needs. Corrections and additions also proved troublesome.

### Mnemonics—a First Step

The first simplification of the programming process came with the use of letters and Arabic numbers in place of basic number codes. The programmer would block out his problem and then use a series of symbols to represent each step in the process. Thus for an instruction such as *load address,* instead of writing 01000001, the programmer need only remember LA. These symbols, or mnemonics, were punched into cards and run through the computer where an assembly program, or processor, translated them into the machine language codes. These translated codes were then punched into cards by the machine to form the program card deck. The deck was then ready to be run with data cards for actual processing of the problem. The technique simplified programming—but it still required one instruction for every step performed by the machine.

This first improvement in programming techniques actually set the stage for all future refinements. For here it was established that the computer, in performing a clerical task —translation of convenient symbols into machine codes—was doing a job the programmer once handled. So, if the computer could perform one programming clerical job, why not others?

It soon became obvious that the processor could take on the added task of assigning storage addresses to data. This data, then, could also be referred to mnemonically—further simplifying the programmer's job. In the early processors, the programmer first assigned a symbolic name and an actual address to an item of data; thereafter he referred to that item by its name. He also indicated where in storage the first instruction was to be placed; other instructions were assigned addresses in sequential locations by the computer, under processor program control.

The next step in expanding the power of programming systems was to eliminate the need for the programmer to specify any of the addresses. He simply indicated how much storage would be required and the processor took over the entire task of allocating storage to data and instructions.

As a result, computers became a lot easier to program. Further evolution of programming expanded on the basic theme of using a prewritten program, or processor, to perform many of the functions formerly requiring manual translation.

### Macros—Another Shortcut

An important characteristic of programming is that certain sequences of instructions are repeated frequently. Over and over, almost any program uses commands to read a card, update a disk file, move a record and so on. Each time they appeared, the programmer had to write and rewrite the series of detailed instructions which told the machine exactly how to go about this particular task.

Here again was another clerical job the computer could do. It led to the development of *macro instructions*—macro, in this case, implying a long sequence of steps. With macro instructions the programmer could write one instruction to, say, "read a tape" and the processor could then automatically insert the corresponding detailed series of machine commands. In this way, the programmer could avoid, for the first time, the task of writing one instruction for every machine step.

While this certainly was a boon to programming, the problem of organizing input-output operations grew. Electronic equipment had progressed to the point where internal processing was measured in millionths of a second, and core storage and disk files were able to hold millions or billions of bits of data. Computers could read, write and compute simultaneously, so the programmer had to work out ways to process more than one record at a time.

To handle the more complex problems of simultaneous operation of the computer and input-output equipment, programmers developed special routines called input-output control systems (IOCS). Basically, an IOCS makes it possible for the programmer to write a problem as if it were a simple sequential operation: get a record, process it, and put the result into an output format. The IOCS program makes it possible to provide the machine language coding necessary to schedule operations, to identify errors, and to provide efficient routines for reading and writing tape, card and disk records.

In addition to input-output control systems, programmers developed other standard programs to take over other repetitive tasks. Programs to sort and merge records, report generators to simplify specification of formats, and utility programs all take clerical burdens off the programmers and put them on the machine.

### Three Branches

While the first computer programmers were, of necessity, jacks-of-all-trades (they had to know machines, programming techniques and applications), programming soon generated its own subspecialties. The first logical division of programming came with the distinction between *applications programming* and *systems programming*. Though there is and probably always will be an overlap, systems programmers write the programs that run the computing equipment while applications programmers write programs that put the computer to work on specific jobs.

An important subdivision of systems programming is programming language development—producing the assemblers, FORTRANS, COBOLS and other translation programs. With programming languages, applications programmers can instruct a computer in a language closer to English and normal mathematical notation than the ones and zeros of machine language. Programming language development, then, is the creation of programs that permit the computer to translate a natural language statement into the numerical, machine-language instructions, or object programs, that actually operate the computer.

These areas of programming—systems programming, language development, and applications programming—are intrinsically interdependent, but the trends in programming will be clarified if we look at the evolution of each separately.

I. *Programming languages.* The development of programming languages began with the development of mnemonic techniques and macroinstructions. If computers could be programmed to translate mnemonic instructions to their numerical equivalents, why couldn't they be programmed to translate more general statements of mathematics and business calculation?

They could and they were. From the base provided by the assembler languages came high-level programming languages such as FORTRAN and COBOL. FORmula TRANslation (FORTRAN) was an IBM development for scientific and engineering problems. Common Business Oriented Language (COBOL) was inspired by the Department of Defense as a machine independent language which would cut across the language boundaries of all computers.

Because earlier computers were designed primarily for either business or scientific computing, the programming languages that emerged during the 1950s and 1960s also reflected this specialization.

However, the difference between scientific and business computing has dimmed. Traditionally, business computers were designed to handle a lot of data on which they performed a limited amount of calculation, while scientific computers performed a lot of computations on relatively small amounts of data.

With the appearance of more sophisticated business problems, such as simulation of marketing plans and production facilities, business computers began to need the high-speed computing ability of scientific computers. Scientists and engineers, on the other hand, found that they could profitably use the commercial computer's talent in manipulating large data files for applications such as test data reduction. The IBM System/360, designed for both business and scientific use, is a prime example of the way in which merging computing requirements of business and science have affected computer design.

Current programming developments also show the trend toward multipurpose systems. One of the most important is PL/1, a language that programmers can use to write instructions for System/360 for use in either scientific or business applications. COBOL and FORTRAN continue to be improved as programming languages.

II. *Systems programming.* From the relatively straightforward job of creating little strings of instructions that directed a computer to read a card and write a tape record, systems programming has evolved into the most complex of programming tasks. The creation of input-output control systems set the direction. Faster and faster computers created the need for ever more efficient workflow. The computer became too fast to depend on human intervention to switch it from job to job, so programmers created monitor or executive programs to help the computer operator keep up with the workflow.

The first IBM monitor program went into operation in 1960 on high-speed scientific computers. Under monitor control, a computer can run almost nonstop through an indefinite series of jobs stacked up in a waiting queue.

When IBM System/360 was created, the development of a monitor control program, or operating system, played as important a part in the system design as did technological developments in electronics circuitry.

Essentially, the operating system uses the decision-making speed of the computer to run routine tasks on the computer with a minimum of operator intervention. The computer is capable of looking for a new job just as it looks for a new instruction within the confines of a single program. The computer can also reallocate its own resources to meet the changing demands of each job.

A typical operating system is equipped with all the compilers—the language translation programs—and special programs that operate input-output equipment. The computer doesn't have to be halted to set up a certain compiler for one job and then another compiler for a subsequent job. The operating system controls all elements and calls them in when needed.

Operating systems add tremendous speed, flexibility and scope to computer-associated communications (Tele-processing) devices. Regardless of the work being performed by the computer at any given time, the operating system monitor can interrupt work in progress and execute programs needed to process incoming messages. When the message or inquiry has been completed, the monitor will then cause work to resume at the point it was interrupted. In larger systems where the capacity is available, Tele-processing may be interleaved with other work.

III. *Applications programming.* The programming developments that led to operating systems and high-order programming languages had two major goals: to make computer programming and operation easier and more efficient. In essence, they are tools to produce and help execute the applications programs that do the actual computing jobs from writing payroll to simulating spacecraft.

In the first years of commercial computing, manufacturers provided little in the way of direct application program assistance. It was felt that users would prefer to—and should —write their own applications programs to reflect their own particular needs or methods of doing business. This is still true to a large extent. Today, however, programmers are often able to start at some advanced point in their programming endeavors, thanks to applications programs supplied and proved out by the manufacturer of the computer.

At IBM, applications programming is a major effort. Its antecedents go back to the 1950s when IBM began developing and training marketing representatives and systems engineers as specialists in specific industries such as aerospace, banking, manufacturing, utilities and insurance. Two things became clear:

1. Certain broad data processing functions common to many companies—despite their individual differences—could be programmed and have applicability throughout industry.

2. Customer companies and their programmers would welcome more specific programming assistance.

IBM's applications programs proliferated: in banking, demand deposit accounting; in finance, portfolio selection; in aerospace, PERT (Program Evaluation and Review Technique); in metals manufacturing, numerical control of machine tools; in publishing, line justification; in education, class scheduling; in wholesale distribution, scientific inventory management. In all, IBM has packaged over 225 applications programs.

### Families of Program Modules

Applications programs for System/360 continue the trend. Many of them will operate under the control of System/360 operating systems.

Applications programs such as the System/360 Advanced Life Information System, Property and Liability Information System, Demand Deposit Accounting and On-Line

Teller Program are actually families of program modules which can be placed in auxiliary storage and called into use by System/360 on an "as needed" basis. The modularity of these programs makes them easier to tailor to specific jobs. Thus, the same kind of progress in the evolution of applications programming is found as in the evolution of systems programming.

### Freeing the Programmer

Programming over the past dozen years has progressed from stand-alone routines designed to perform one job at a time to hierarchies of programs in Operating System/360. Operating systems will relieve the programmer of many problems, freeing him to concentrate on the primary task of problem solution. Using applications programs, he may be able to start with a large part of his task programmed and pretested.

What about the future? Certainly as computers get faster, input-output devices more numerous, and problems still more complicated, the major trends in programming development will continue to provide better, simpler and more efficient ways for computers to solve problems. This steady accumulation and improvement of programming is the key to the computer's constantly growing utility.

### SOLVING A PROBLEM [4]

How does the computer solve a problem? In very much the same way that you do.

Let's take a problem. You're paymaster of the Supersonic Hubcap Company. You want to figure out how much to pay one employee, George Geargrinder, for last week's work. You ask your secretary to check the pay records and bring you certain information: how many hours Mr. Geargrinder worked last week, how much he earns an hour, and his pay-

[4] From pamphlet, "You and the Computer: A Student's Guide," General Electric Company. 570 Lexington Ave. New York 10022. '65. p 5-7. © 1965 by the General Electric Company. Reprinted by permission.

roll deductions. She checks the records and reports that Mr. Geargrinder worked 35 hours. His rate of pay is $3 an hour. His deductions are 15 per cent for income tax and $1 for insurance.

With these facts you can easily figure out George Geargrinder's wages. First, find gross pay by multiplying the hours he worked by his rate of pay. This comes to $105. Now figure the deductions: income tax is 15 per cent of $105, or $15.75; add $1 for health insurance and you get a total of $16.75. Subtract these deductions from $105 gross pay, and you end up with $88.25, which is Mr. Geargrinder's take-home pay. Write him a check for this amount.

In working this problem you performed five main functions. The computer performs the same five functions. They are:

*Input.* This is getting the facts in hand so you can use them. Your secretary performed an input function when she gave you Mr. Geargrinder's pay records. With a computer, you also feed in basic information so it can work the problem.

*Storage.* This is keeping the pertinent information available for ready use in working a problem. The computer has a memory in which it stores both information for solving a problem and instructions on how to use the information.

*Calculation.* You solved this problem with an adding machine; you might have used a pencil and paper. The computer's calculating, or arithmetic, unit operates on the same principles as an adding machine. It can add, subtract, multiply, and divide.

*Output.* After you gathered your facts and worked the necessary arithmetic, you had the answer. George Geargrinder was due $88.25 in wages, so you wrote him a check. This was output. For the computer, output is the act of taking answers out of the computer after the problem has been worked.

*Control.* Control simply means doing things in proper order. When you work a problem, you subconsciously do first things first: look at records, find hours worked, write on paper, and so forth. The computer must be guided every step of the way. This is the job of the computer's control unit.

Obviously you don't need a computer if your only job is to figure out one man's wages. But suppose as paymaster of Supersonic Hubcap Company you have to figure out the wages for ten thousand employees! For this you need the help of a computer. For a computer, working automatically, can calculate the wages and write paychecks for ten thousand persons in a single day.

## "Basic" Computer at Work

The heart of the computer's ability to work automatically is its ability to remember instructions as well as facts.

The computer's memory can be compared to a block of post-office boxes, where each box holds one person's mail. In the computer's memory each "box" holds one item of information, either a fact or an instruction. In the computer these "boxes" are called memory locations.

With some post-office boxes as the memory, a blackboard as the calculating section, and a mechanical hand to control the movement of data and instructions, we have a basic computer.

Let's see if we can have our computer calculate the wages of Supersonic Hubcap Company's ten thousand employees and issue their checks.

First, we need input, which in this case is payroll facts. Previously prepared time cards—one for each employee—will provide such facts. We place these cards in an input machine that loads payroll facts on one employee at a time into the computer's memory.

We must decide in which memory locations to store each fact. Each memory location has its own identifying number called an address. Let's put the employee's name in address 13; hours worked in address 14; rate of pay in address 15; percentage of income tax deduction in address 16, and health insurance deduction in address 17....

Now we can write a series of instructions that will automatically figure the pay of George Geargrinder, or any other
person whose pay facts are loaded into the computer.

We will store the instructions in the computer's memory
in exactly the same way we stored the pay facts. It doesn't
make any difference which boxes we use, as all are equally
accessible. Let's put the first instruction in box number 0.

| *Address* | *Instruction* |
|---|---|
| 0 | Write contents of address 14 (hours worked) on blackboard. |
| 1 | Multiply contents of address 15 (rate of pay) times number on blackboard. |
| 2 | Copy previous answer into address 18 (but don't erase it from blackboard) . |
| 3 | Multiply contents of address 16 (percentage of income tax deduction) times previous answer. |
| 4 | Add contents of address 17 to previous answer. |
| 5 | Subtract previous answer from contents of address 18 (gross pay) . |
| 6 | Write a paycheck for the amount of previous answer. |
| 7 | Make check out to contents of address 13 (name of employee) . |
| 8 | Load information about next employee into memory locations 13, 14, 15, 16 and 17. (Loading new data into memory automatically erases information previously there.) |
| 9 | Start over by following instructions in address 0. |

To get our computer started on the payroll, we can set it
at address number 0, just as we might set the hands of a clock.
After following the instruction in address 0, the computer
will automatically move forward, one address at a time, carrying out each instruction as it goes. The last instruction—

stored in address 9—resets the computer at address 0, thus automatically starting the operation all over again.

A real computer doesn't have mechanical hands. Instead it has electronic connections that carry information at nearly the speed of light (186,000 miles per second). Thus, you can see how the computer could easily figure out a payroll thousands of times faster than you could, working by hand.

When all ten thousand employees have been paid, we remove payroll instructions from the computer's memory and store them for future use in coded form on cards or tape. Then we can put in a different set of instructions and do a different job. For instance, we might put in a program that decides how many hubcaps we should manufacture in the next month. Along with this new program, we would put into the computer all the required data—sales reports from regional offices, number of hubcaps already on hand, etc.— and start the machine. In the same methodical, step-by-step way, the computer would come up with the month's manufacturing requirements.

## HOW THE COMPUTER IS USED [5]

### By a Hospital Floor Nurse

A hospital floor nurse receives automatic reminder messages on the typewriter terminal at her nursing station to follow through on doctor's orders for medication and patient care. In addition, after the doctor has entered orders for tests, special foods or drugs at the station, the computer sends necessary information to laboratory technicians, the kitchen and the pharmacy. Each of the five hundred nurses at this hospital spends an estimated 40 per cent of her time— more than three hours a day—doing paperwork. By substituting a data terminal for multiple paper forms, the nursing

[5] From pamphlet, "The Computer Comes of Age." International Business Machines Corporation. Data Processing Division. 112 E. Post Rd. White Plains, N.Y. 10601. (no date) p 9-11. Reprinted by permission.

supervisor reports that the computer has increased the effective nursing time by about 20 per cent, the same as hiring another one hundred nurses.

### By an Airline Reservations Clerk

An airline reservations clerk in Chicago places a card listing all flights to a given city on a display rack, then presses a button on a special terminal to request flight information for a potential passenger. The request is relayed to the airline's central computer which searches its file and indicates to the agent whether space is available. The space is then confirmed by entering the passenger's name and other information on the terminal. Seat availability is automatically adjusted for that particular flight. All this is done within a matter of seconds. . . .

### By an Automotive Test Engineer

An automotive test engineer steps into a new car in a quality inspection laboratory to start an exhaust emission test, in which exhaust gases are analyzed with respect to governmental standards for air pollution control. After analysis equipment is hooked to the exhaust pipe, the computer triggers a tape-recorded voice instructing the driver to start the car, idle the engine and then accelerate to various speeds. As the car's rear wheels spin on rollers, exhaust samples are analyzed by the computer and the results sent to the appropriate plant areas for any necessary corrective action.

### By a Refinery Engineer

A refinery engineer enters information on prices of petroleum products, as well as on physical and chemical properties of the raw petroleum input, into a computer model of a catalytic cracking unit. The computer manipulates the data to determine the most economical way to produce the specified liquid petroleum gas and other oil products on the basis of the shifting market demand and the process variables.

The computer also controls the complex process of petroleum distillation to insure the most profitable production.

## By a Railroad Yardmaster

A railroad yardmaster can at any instant ask for up-to-date information on the location of any freight car in the railroad's system. At the same time, a nearby computer terminal automatically prints out a list that tells in sequence what cars are arriving at his yard. With knowledge of the existing yard situation, he can determine where cars should be switched for fastest possible movement to their ultimate destination. The railroad's computer system for freight car location encompasses more than seventy traffic and yard offices and fifty shippers' offices in twenty-seven states.

## By a Policeman

A policeman radios or telephones a suspicious-looking vehicle's license number into local headquarters. A request for information on a possible stolen vehicle is typed into a terminal and relayed to the National Crime Information Center in Washington, D.C. If the car was stolen, confirmation is flashed back to the requesting terminal, together with a description of the vehicle and other identifying information. In less than three minutes, the policeman on the scene has enough information to stop the vehicle and check the driver. The 95,000 crime records in the NCIC system—stolen vehicles, stolen license plates, stolen and missing guns and wanted persons—are supplied and used by cooperating police departments throughout the United States.

## By a Stockbroker

A stockbroker at a trading post on the floor of the New York Stock Exchange records the details of a transaction on a special card, designating stock symbol, number of shares and price. The card is placed in a data reader at the trading post, which scans the pencil marks and transmits the information to the Exchange's computer center. The data is verified and immediately transmitted by telegraph to some 3,800 stock tickers in the United States and Canada. Using a telephone quotation service, the stockbroker can also telephone the computer center, dial a four-digit code for any of 1,500 stocks listed on the Exchange, and receive a verbal statement of the latest price.

### In the Future

There are more than fifty thousand computers in operation throughout the world today. It has been predicted that the number will expand to 85,000 by 1975, and to date all such predictions have proved to be conservative. Amazing as this growth may be, the most significant progress has been in the evolution of the computer as a familiar tool—rather than an electronic marvel. More and more people are using the computer in exciting new ways, and its future is limited only by the imagination of its users.

## THE ANALOG COMPUTER [6]

The world of electronic computation encompasses more than one species.

It has been inhabited for two decades not only by the digital computer but also by the analog computer. In addition, there is a flourishing newcomer, the hybrid computer, which combines the strong features of both the digital and analog machines.

Basically, an analog computer consists of an assembly of individual electronic computing elements that can be interconnected by means of a "patch panel" outside the machine. This panel is a terminal board with holes, each hole facing an internal contact. The computer operator uses "patch cords" (wire connectors) to interconnect specific holes for the kind of operation he wants the machine to perform.

[6] From article, "For Easy Rapport Between Man and Machine There's Nothing Quite Like an Analog Computer," by Robert Vichnevetsky, manager of research and advanced development, Electronic Associates, Inc. New York *Times.* p C 140. Ja. 6, '69. © 1969 by The New York Times Company. Reprinted by permission.

The primary electronic components inside the analog computer include parts resembling those found in more familiar electronic equipment, like a radio or a television set. But they are used differently. When arranged in certain configurations, the parts can be used to reproduce an information flow corresponding to the mathematical equations of a real-life dynamic process or system.

The fundamental element of analog computers is the operational amplifier, a combination of transistors with the capability for very great signal gain. Such an amplifier can be used to perform various mathematical operations, depending on which particular circuit is connected into a "feedback path" leading back from the output end of the amplifier to its input side.

Unlike a digital computer, which is programmed to operate step by step, the analog computer processes information continuously. This information is contained in the variations of electrical voltages that represent the dynamics of the problem to be solved.

A basic voltage range, say, from –10 volts to +10 volts, is designed into the machine and imposes the voltage limits within which it operates. This standard range can be scaled to make it conform conveniently to the range of the quantities to be processed. One volt, for example, may be chosen to represent, say, five feet, 200 pounds or .01 degree.

Besides the individual computing elements, the analog computer has an overall control (pushbuttons, dials and switches) that permits the operator to control the computation performed by the machine as it goes along. The results of the analog computer's work are normally not numbers, but curves that can be read on various types of recording apparatus connected at the output of the machine.

In this respect, a perceptive technologist once drove home the difference between analog and digital devices with a memorable illustration. He pointed out that the analog man thinks of the female form as a curvaceous outline while the digital man thinks of 36-24-36.

Like the digital computer, the analog computer—functioning differently—can add, subtract, multiply and divide. But arithmetic is not what the analog computer is used for primarily.

It is used basically as a research-and-development tool to simulate a large variety of dynamic systems that are found in industrial research and many other scientific disciplines.

The analog computer lends itself to research and development in a way that allows a close man-machine relationship between the analyst using it and the system he is trying to analyze. Once the computer has been programmed to simulate a system, the analyst can play with that system as if it were a real one and make adjustments in it to improve its performance before the system is actually built.

Originally, analog computers were used mainly by the aircraft industry to solve difficult engineering problems. Shortly thereafter, their use spread to many other segments of industry for such purposes as analyzing the behavior of nuclear reactors, evaluating automobile wheel-suspension systems and simulating the performance of the various complex elements involved in the operations of large chemical plants.

Essentially, an analog computer simulates a real process by means of differential equations that are set up for the machine by the connections that the operator makes at the patch panel mentioned above. Such equations establish exact relationships between physical quantities and their rates of change.

Differential equations set up in the machine are exactly the same as those that describe the behavior of the system itself. Therefore, the machine simulates the system by analogy, which explains why it is called an analog computer.

Digital computers can be programmed to solve almost any problem that analog computers can solve. But it is impossible to evaluate their relative merits without introducing factors concerning machine speed and the degree of flexibility with which a scientist can modify his instructions to the computer if he wants to make changes.

The complexity of scientific problems sometimes makes a digital computer extremely slow because of the astronomical number of elementary operations that it is called upon to perform sequentially. On the other hand, the analog computer is not burdened by the complexity of such problems because it operates dynamically and continuously in a nonsequential manner.

One of the major problems in the operation of a computer is the relationship between the machine and the man who uses it. Such a relationship is described by the word *interface*. *Interface* is a general term applied when two different systems or a system and a man have to operate together.

From the engineering user's standpoint, a digital computer is sometimes difficult to interface with. Analog computers are easy to interface with, but they sometimes lack the accuracy that digital computers have. Furthermore, their memory capability is limited.

Bringing together the best offered by both machines is what has been achieved by hybrid computers. In the hybrid machine, the "translation" link is provided by connecting elements known as analog-to-digital and digital-to-analog converters.

Analog and hybrid computers now have wide applications. They are being used as educational aids and in industry and science for such primary purposes as evaluating new proposed systems or controls, establishing better operating techniques for existing systems and training persons to operate such systems.

# III. HOW DID THE COMPUTER COME ABOUT?

## EDITOR'S INTRODUCTION

Although the modern computer is of recent vintage its history spans many centuries. To understand fully how it came about one must go all the way back to that period when man first invented numbers—for it is numbers, of course, that the computer uses in solving problems.

The first selection in this section looks at the origins of numbers and explains how they relate to logic and how this relationship forms the basic theoretical framework on which computers work.

Once numbers had been mastered, man began to look for instruments that would facilitate and speed up making mathematical calculations. the next selection recounts the history of computing devices and their gradual evolution into the fairly sophisticated machines that could honestly be called computers.

Interestingly, many of the underlying theories for a computer had been formed more than a century ago by Charles Babbage, an English mathematical genius. But unfortunately for him the equipment available to him was too clumsy to match his ideas. Indeed, it wasn't until 1948 that a group of Bell Telephone Laboratories scientists invented a transistor—a small device for handling electrical current. More than any other single invention the transistor made possible computers small enough, and reliable enough, to be genuinely functional. The third article, written just about the time transistors were being made for widespread use in 1952, explains how transistors came about and how they work. By 1956 their use and importance had so proliferated that John Bardeen, Walter H. Brattain, and William Shockley, the three scientists who invented them, were honored with a Nobel prize in physics.

The modern computer is essentially an electronic machine, with no mechanical gears for calculations. The era began with the construction of ENIAC, the Electronic Numerical Integrator and Computer. The final selection in this section charts the history of computers from the time of ENIAC into the late 1950s and early 1960s. From that point on, as noted in Section I, computer use, the growth of the computer industry, and the impact of the computer on our society have been nothing short of explosive.

## LOGIC AS A BASE [1]

The story of how man learned to count is buried in the distant past, thousands of years before written records of any kind existed. At some time in man's history a great intellectual leap was made. Exactly how we do not know; perhaps a primitive man was looking at the food he had collected for storing against the winter. He knew that there were "many" or at any rate "more than one" individual items. Suddenly, a marvelous idea occurred to him. His hands, which had labored to gather his food, were two ready-made calculating machines. By holding up or touching one finger for each item in the piles of food before him, he could find a way to say how many things there were. The fruit he had saved might equal all the fingers on one hand plus the thumb of the other; the pile of nuts might have as many nuts in it as he had fingers on both hands and toes on both feet.

This concept that the number of things there are is independent of what kinds of things are counted—a group of nine apples and a group of nine eggs have in common only that there are nine things in each group—is one of the most important man ever arrived at.

[1] From *Man, Memory, and Machines—An Introduction to Cybernetics*, by Corinne Jacker, author and science editor. Macmillan. '64. p 30-41. Reprinted with permission of The Macmillan Company from *Man, Memory, and Machines*, by Corinne Jacker. Copyright © by Corinne Jacker 1964.

Our word *digit*—any number under ten—comes from the Latin *digitus*, which means finger. In fact, the German historian and archaeologist Theodor Mommsen (1817-1903) was struck by the visual significance of the lower Roman numerals. I (or 1 in our numerical system) might clearly be a symbol for one finger held up; V (or 5) could be a kind of pictorial representation of an open hand held with the thumb spread far apart from the fingers. Then X (10) would be two of these.

Our numerical system, the *decimal system*, has a *base* of 10. A base is the number on which a mathematical system is constructed—its basis—and in the digital system all mathematical operations are based on the number 10. It may be that we have chosen this base because there are ten fingers (including the thumbs) on our two hands. In some parts of the world, though, men thought that if counting on their fingers was efficient, counting on both fingers and toes would be even better. So they developed the vigesimal system, with the number 20 as its base. Even today this system can still be found among some Eskimo, American Indian, and African tribes. It was also the mathematical basis for the great Aztec and Mayan civilizations of Mexico and Central America. Not all systems have had this simple origin; the Babylonian system, for example, had a base of 60, which could have no apparent physiological basis. Although some systems may have speed or ease of calculation to recommend them, none is inherently better than the rest, or more natural.

Another way of looking at our hands in order to use them in counting is to think of the whole hand as a unit. In this way, the system would have a base of 2. This is called the *binary system*, and is the language of electronic computers. The binary system is still very much used by people too, and it is easy to see how natural such a system is: we have two hands, two eyes, two feet, two ears. Some Australian aborigines—the Kulin Kurrai of the southeast and the Narrinyeri of the south—and the tribes on both sides of the Torres Strait, which separates Australia and New Guinea, count in this way, as do the Bushmen of Africa and some of the oldest tribes of South America. [The German genius Gottfried Wilhelm] Leibniz . . . was struck by the elegance of the binary system, and was the first modern mathematician to concern himself with it.

There is an excellent reason why a computer uses the binary system and not any other, although in some ways it might be simpler if we and the computer did our mathematics in the same way. The electronic computer uses electricity, and one important fact about an electrical current is that it can be shut off and turned on again. In effect, the most widely used type of computer—the *digital computer*—has two hands but no fingers, so the most logical and economical system is the binary one: on or off, 1 or 0, yes or no. The nervous system, too, operates with an on-off electrical pulse signal, transmitting its messages in a kind of binary code. . . .

In most information-communication systems, the information is transmitted by signals of some sort, such as the dots and dashes of the Morse Code; but the silences between the dots and dashes do not communicate anything; they are wasted. However, since the two numbers of the binary system can be considered equal to the on (1) and off (0) signals of electric current, no flow of current conveys just as much information as a flow: both supply one of the two binary digits. If one wanted to, one could also refer to the two possibilities as yes and no. And this opens a whole new area of computer uses, since it would then be possible for the computer, given proper instructions, to say yes or no in answer to a question. Then, assuming that a logic or system of reasoning was based on this concept, it would be possible for a computer to reason. Such a system does exist.

It is not as hard to reduce the complexities of human thought to yes-or-no quantities as one might think. The English mathematician and logician George Boole (1815-1864) developed a kind of *mathematical logic* that has proved to be ideal for computer use. In 1854 he published his great work, *An Investigation of the Laws of Thought,* which described this logic.

First, it was Boole's idea that many statements are of the same kind although they refer to very different particular things. He felt that statements could be reduced to quantities, like the $x$'s and $y$'s used in algebra to represent unknown quantities. Let us take two very different statements:

1. If the temperature of water rises above 212 degrees Fahrenheit, then water will begin to boil.
2. If I have enough money at the end of the week, then I will go to a movie.

Now in the first statement, let $x$ equal "the temperature of water rises above 212 degrees Fahrenheit," and let $y$ equal "the water will begin to boil." We get a new statement, "If $x$, then $y$."

Taking the second statement and making a similar substitution, we let $x$ equal "I have enough money at the end of the week," and $y$ equals "I will go to a movie." The statement then becomes "If $x$, then $y$." So the statements both have become:

1. If $x$, then $y$.
2. If $x$, then $y$.

This means that, although they are talking about two very different things, the same logical inference may be drawn from each of them: if $x$ is true, then $y$ will be true. Boole showed that, no matter what the content of a statement is, if it is in the form of "if $x$, then $y$," the same logical inference is made by it as by any and all other statements of the same type. Boole also showed that these quantities to which the statements are reduced can be manipulated mathematically, in the same way as algebraic $x$'s and $y$'s can be handled.

Incidentally, when looking at statements in this general way it is important to keep them within their limits. Take, for example, the positive and negative for statement 2:

2a. If I have enough money at the end of the week, then I will go to a movie.

We have to assume that this statement is logically true, because it has been made. That is, for the purposes of logic, whether the person who made that statement is telling a lie or not does not matter, but

2b. If I do not have enough money at the end of the week, then I will not go to a movie.

while it may be true practically is not necessarily logically true. This becomes obvious when other possibilities are considered. Although I may have no money left at the end of the week, I may still go to the movies because my father may give me the money, my brother may treat me, or—if I am a girl—I may have a date on Saturday night and be taken to the movies. Let us put this into a kind of mathematical shorthand. Let $-x$ be the negative or opposite of $x$: "I do not have enough money at the end of the week," and let $-y$ be: "I will not go to a movie." We already have the statement:

If $x$, then $y$.
Suppose $-x$ is the case. Logically we cannot say:

If $x$, then $y$.
$-x$, so $-y$.

Thus it is possible to handle a statement as a mathematical quantity, but—as in mathematics—there are rules for its manipulation. And it must be remembered that when the logician talks about true and false he is talking about statements that are logically true and false. Mathematical logic may use statements that are complete nonsense or statements that have been made by liars. "If Napoleon becomes President of the United States, then I will be a millionaire" is nonsense. But it is still an "if $x$, then $y$" type of statement. The logician can only take it and other statements, analyze them logically, and draw conclusions that are logically sound. He cannot as a logician distinguish in any philosophical or moral way between true and false, good and bad.

Essentially, then, mathematical logic is a kind of binary logic, because it is based on the premise that statements are logically either true or false, yes or no, 1 or 0. And a computer, if it is properly programmed, is an expert at mathematical logic. If a programmer wanted to put the information in the statement "If I have enough money at the end of the week, then I will go to a movie" into a computer, he could look at the shorthand we used above (if *x*, then *y*) and use the binary system instead. He could say that *x* would be programmed, with 10 arbitrarily chosen to represent *x*, as 10 – 1; – *x* could then be programmed as 10 – 0. The computer could then take this statement, along with a number of others, and perform the mathematical operations of a special kind of algebra called Boolean algebra.

As a matter of fact, about fifteen years after Boole published his work, an English economist and logician, William Stanley Jevons (1835-1882), built and exhibited a logical machine that operated according to principles Boole had set down.

In 1938, the American mathematician Claude Shannon, then of MIT (Massachusetts Institute of Technology), published an article, "A Symbolic Analysis of Relay and Switching Circuits," in the *Transactions of the American Institute of Electrical Engineers*. This very vital technical paper related Boolean algebra to electrical circuits and the programming of computers.

## EARLY HISTORY [2]

Computer development as we now see it is primarily a phenomenon of the twentieth century. Nevertheless, a historical record of mechanical computing aids stretches back many centuries, and is inextricably tied up with man's basic urge to count, to quantify, and to measure. Our very word *counter*, referring to the board over which we buy and sell merchandise, goes back to the time when it had built into it a mechanical aid for reckoning the bill. The earliest such counting devices probably consisted of strings of beads or shells. With the invention of formal numbering systems, simple counters of this sort developed into a very useful calculating device called the *abacus*. Its basic design has changed little in the past several thousand years and it is still in wide use throughout the world. We may better appreciate the universal social influence of the abacus by remembering that the English words *calculate* and *calculus* are derived from the beads or *calculi* used on the wires of the abacus. It is by no means a trivial computing aid. A skillful user of the abacus can frequently keep ahead of electric desk calculators.

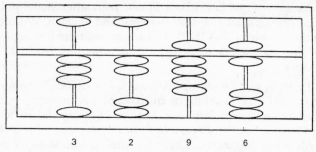

3       2       9       6

*Drawing of Japanese Abacus or Soroban*
*Beads Are Set to Represent the Number 3296*

It is instructive to consider how numbers can be represented on an abacus. Refer to the schematic in [the above] figure . . . where each column of beads represents one digit position and is divided by the horizontal bar into a lower group of four and a single upper bead. The upper bead is worth five units in its column position; each bead in the lower group is worth one unit. To represent any digit from 1 through 4, the corresponding number of beads in the lower group is moved into position just beneath and adjacent to the divider bar. To represent 5, the upper bead is moved down to a position just above the divider bar and all the lower beads are returned to the bottom of the frame. The digit 6 is represented by the upper bead and one of the lower beads brought into position nearest the divider bar. To go from digit 9 to 10 requires a left carry of one unit that must be accounted for manually by adjusting one or more beads in the next position to the left.

## The Antikythera Device

We shall often use the word *digital* as descriptive of modern electronic computers. The abacus is also a digital device since its principles of operation depend on the use of a formal system of counting. In general, all digital computers share this property with the abacus. A digital computer is a calculating device that carries out its computations by manipulating the counting digits of a number system. There is, however, a basically different kind of computer that we mention here for reasons of completeness and of historical interest. This kind of device is called an *analog* computer. Its principle of operation depends on the measurement of smoothly varying physical quantities. Ancient examples of analog devices are the hourglass and the sundial. In the latter, the smoothly changing position of the sun's shadow on the graduated periphery of a brass dial provides an estimate of the time of day. Other familiar devices illustrating both analog and digital principles are the speedometer and odometer used in automobiles. The speedometer is an analog computer. It receives an input from a rotating wheel connected to the car's drive shaft and provides an output in the form of a pointer whose position varies smoothly against a graduated dial. The odometer receives the same input from the drive shaft but provides a digital output in the form of a counter whose readings give distance in miles and tenths of a mile. It can be looked at as a small, special-purpose digital computer, though it involves a conversion of the analog input into a digital output. Sometimes, computing devices involving both analog and digital principles are called *hybrid* computers.

Surprisingly enough, the Greeks had built a sophisticated analog computer one hundred years before the birth of Christ. In 1901 Dodecanese sponge divers were driven by rough weather to anchor in an unaccustomed location off the Greek island of Antikythera in the Mediterranean Sea. There, in about two hundred feet of water, they discovered the wreck of an ancient ship containing articles of trade, including many bronze and marble statues. Much of the statuary was in fragments and what was at first believed to be some of the broken pieces turned out to be parts of a clock-like mechanism containing a complex array of gears, slip rings, rods, and other components. The entire device had been in happier times enclosed in a wooden box with hinged doors. On the face of the box were graduated scales and rings with pointers driven by the enclosed machinery. It very much resembled an eighteenth-century clock.

It took several decades to reconstruct a view of the device since the corrosion of sea water left little to build from. But of the original mechanism at least twenty-odd gears were discernible including a very sophisticated assembly of gears mounted eccentrically on a turntable. These probably functioned as a so-called epicyclic differential gear system. It was even found that one of the gears and a shaft had been mended during the life of the instrument.

There is little doubt that the Antikythera Device was used for computing the motions of the heavenly bodies, predicting eclipses and such. It was a primitive form of an orrery or planetarium. Inscriptions on the graduated dials include the names of the sun and of the planet Venus. In particular, there were adjustable slip rings to allow for the ¼ day per year error in the Egyptian calendar on which its operation was evidently based. The slip rings were found set in such a way as to adjust for an error corresponding to about the year 80 B.C., which is in close agreement with date estimates based on analysis of the statuary and other items brought up from the ship. Discovery of the Antikythera Device called for an upward revision of our ideas about Greek technological development. It seems to have been a great deal more advanced than was previously believed. It is interesting to speculate on what present science would be like had the Greek civilization not declined as it did. Another mechanism like the Antikythera computer was not built by men for many centuries.

## Pascal and Leibniz

It was not until the scientific renaissance of the seventeenth century that another step was taken toward mechanized calculation. In 1642 a nineteen-year-old genius named Blaise Pascal wearied of the burdensome arithmetic that fell his lot as an assistant in his father's tax office. Pressed for relief, he built a small mechanical adding device consisting of a number of toothed wheels mounted in a box. Each wheel had ten teeth and each tooth stood for one of the digits 0 through 9. When any one of the wheels passed from position 9 to position 0, a small projection on it would move the next wheel to the left just one position, thus providing an automatic carry. This was the principal innovation of Pascal's device. The same design is used today on paper-tape adding machines. Whereas Pascal's invention caused quite a stir of interest in its day and a model was even presented to the king of France, a practical adding machine awaited a long succession of necessary developments. Pascal's interest in his own invention disappeared as he matured into other phases of his outstanding career as scientist, philosopher, and inventor.

Gottfried Wilhelm Leibniz, the German mathematician and philosopher, engaged in (and lost) at least one problem-solving contest with the English mathematician Isaac Newton. Along with Newton, Leibniz is ranked as one of the two most influential thinkers of the seventeenth century. One of his many accomplishments was the invention of an improved calculating device patterned after Pascal's. Like Pascal, he too was motivated to build his machine to get relief from burdensome computation which he saw as an unproductive occupation for a creative scientific mind. The operation of his device depended on a unique stepped-cylinder arrangement that made it possible to multiply by successive additions. Leibniz' calculator, like Pascal's, was not a practical device, but it is noteworthy for having introduced mechanical ideas important in later, practical machines.

About one hundred years after Leibniz' work, a practical though crude four-process (addition, subtraction, multiplication, and division) calculator was actually built in Germany by a man named Hahn. A further development of Hahn's machine, still a variation of the stepped-cylinder idea of Leibniz, was brought out in 1820. Copies of this machine appeared all over Europe. Its arrival in the United States stimulated further practical improvements, leading gradually to desk-type calculators resembling those in use today.

The Pascal-Leibniz beginning led through a succession of developments to a specific kind of manually operated arithmetic device represented by modern keyboard adding machines. However, it is important to observe that these machines cannot be considered direct ancestors of automatic computers. Adding machines and automatic computers have a common ancestry of course, but while the stepped-cylinder idea was being refined into a workable manual calculator, a completely new line of development was introduced by a brilliant, inventive Englishman named Charles Babbage. It is irresistible to spend a few lines telling about this fascinating man and his remarkable ideas. For it is with Babbage that many fundamentally useful computing concepts had their first expression.

### Charles Babbage

Babbage was born on December 16, 1792; he was the son of a prominent banker who later left him a considerable fortune. From his earliest childhood he had an inquisitive and ingenious turn of mind. It is reported that he eviscerated his toys to see how they worked. To prove whether the devil really existed, he once attempted to invoke him by drawing a circle on the floor with his own blood and reciting the

Lord's prayer backwards. Such striking elements of personal character persisted throughout his life and contributed in no small measure to his omnivorous scientific appetite and his drive to succeed in the goals he set for himself.

During his student days, Babbage became very interested in the error-free computation of numerical tables. For those of us whose daily pursuits normally do not require the use of such tables, the whole topic may seem unnecessary and revoltingly dry. But the importance of various kinds of tables in business, commerce, and science can hardly be overestimated. They are essential in surveying, architecture, navigation, and accounting. In Babbage's day and before, governments of many countries commissioned at great cost the computation by hand and then the publication of voluminous tables of products, powers, roots, and reciprocals of numbers; of interest, discount, and annuities payments; and particularly of astronomical predictions essential to safe navigation. Almost everyone has heard the expression "shooting the sun" in reference to determining a ship's position at sea. Nautical tables give hour-by-hour positions for the sun and other bodies the navigator uses to compare with his observations and determine his current latitude and longitude at sea. A table of day-by-day positions for a heavenly body is called an *ephemeris*. Even isolated errors in a nautical ephemeris can prove catastrophic. There is the story of a ship that went aground off Lizard Head because of such an error. The ship's log showing the erroneously reckoned position and the almanac containing the incorrect figures were brought up from the captain's cabin. Subsequent editions of the offending tables included corrections for the wrong entries but, as someone remarked, it seems a desperately extravagant way of developing error-free tables.

In some forty volumes of tables selected from a library in 1834, no less than 3,700 errors were acknowledged by the presence of inserted corrections. In one instance, some important nautical tables for finding latitude and longitude at sea were computed, revised, rerevised, and published with utmost care under the direction of the British government and even then were found to contain more than one thousand incorrect entries. Many governments spared no expense to achieve accuracy in tables. The young French republic aspired to lead the world in every way, including production of the best numerical tables possible. To that end, G. F. Prony was commissioned to carry out the task. Prony's approach was to divide the labor among three groups of workers. The first group were leading mathematicians who chose the proper formulas and procedures. The second group were qualified mathematicians who organized the computation into prescribed sequences of arithmetic steps. The third group were human computers who knew nothing but the four operations of arithmetic. Unfortunately, though Prony's tables were excellent, they were never published, partly because of turning tides of political fortune. But it was observed later that the workers responsible for the fewest mistakes were the computers in group three. What Prony attempted with human components, Babbage proposed to carry out entirely by machine. One report has it that on finding numerous mistakes in a numerical table prepared for the Astronomical Society, Babbage exclaimed, "I wish to God these calculations had been executed by steam!" His desire to accomplish this end determined the major course of his life.

## The Difference Engine

Babbage proposed the machine computation of tables by using only the operation of addition. It is not difficult to understand what he had in mind. Consider the table of squares in [the following] figure . . . which includes additional columns of differences between successive squares and differences between successive differences.

The differences between successive tabular entries are called first differences, differences between successive differences are called second differences, and so on. Notice that for the table of squares, the column of second differences is constant at the value 2. After discovering this property of second differences for squares, we may calculate further squares from the preceding entries by using only addition. The amount we must add to any square to get the next will clearly be 2 more than the difference between the two preceding squares. Another way to describe the computation is

| Number | Square | First difference | Second difference |
|--------|--------|------------------|-------------------|
| 1 | 1 | | |
| 2 | 4 | 3 | 2 |
| 3 | 9 | 5 | 2 |
| 4 | 16 | 7 | 2 |
| 5 | 25 | 9 | 2 |
| 6 | 36 | 11 | 2 |
| 7 | 49 | 13 | 2 |
| 8 | 64 | 15 | 2 |
| 9 | 81 | 17 | |

*Difference Table for Successive Squares*

as follows: Extend the second-differences column as far as desired. Then extend the first-differences column by adding the corresponding second-difference value at each step. Then extend the squares column by adding the appropriate first-difference entry at each step. Now, as it happens, almost all tables can be prepared by this method of differences, though the order and value of the constant-difference column must be determined for the table to be prepared. What Babbage proposed to build was a mechanical device into which the order and value of the constant difference could be set and which would then proceed to generate as many table entries as desired by a process of repeated additions. Because it used a process depending on properties of differences, Babbage called his machine a Difference Engine.

In 1822 Babbage set down a rough outline of his first model consisting of some eighteen wheels and three axes. He published an article on the machine calculation of tables and communicated his ideas in a letter to Sir Humphrey

Davy, president of the Royal Society. Babbage pointed out the potential advantages for the government if a Difference Engine could be built. What he actually proposed to build was a Difference Engine of twenty-place accuracy for operating with differences up to the sixth order. After being set for production of a specified table, it would automatically stamp the successive entries into an engraver's plate for printing directly, without the need for error-prone hand setting into movable type. His plan was truly on a grand scale. Because of its interest in Babbage's proposal, the English government agreed to its support, but, as it turns out, under terms that were never very well understood either by Babbage or the government. In all, the government advanced some £17,000 for the enterprise and Babbage contributed a similar amount from his private fortune. But no more than a fragment of the Difference Engine was ever completed. There are several reasons for the failure of the project, but the most important is that no machine even approximating such complexity had ever been built before. Babbage had to contribute directly to the still self-conscious mechanical technology of his day even to hope for success. There were few standard machine parts and certainly no available processes for mass-producing gears, wheels, cams, links, shafts, and ratchets in the quantity and precision required for the Difference Engine. In clockmaking and other mechanical construction, hand fitting was the usual procedure. The complexity of the required mechanism was simply beyond the available means.

Now it should be clear that the Difference Engine was a special machine just for the automatic computation of tables. During its development and construction, however, Babbage began to see the possibility of designing a general-purpose machine whose capabilities would transcend the Difference Engine in many ways. Because he was convinced that his new and still grander computing machine would, if brought to reality, determine the future course of mathematical analysis, Babbage called it an Analytical Engine. Curiously enough, the genesis of the Analytical Engine and some key features of its ultimate design depended on the prior development of a quite unrelated mechanical contrivance already in practical use in Babbage's day. This device was the automatic loom. Before describing the Analytical Engine and its foreshadowing of concepts important in modern computers, we must digress for a moment to explain how the automatic loom influenced Babbage's ideas.

## The Jacquard Loom

As early as 1661, an unknown genius set up a mechanized loom in the city of Danzig. It was claimed that this machine could automatically weave cloth night and day without human aid. City officials, however, afraid for the jobs of hand-weavers, suppressed the invention and privately drowned the inventor. But despite the continued rather chilly reception to such machines, automatic-loom devices appeared from time to time during the next century, leading to the Jacquard card-driven loom patented in France in 1801.

A fundamental step in the weaving process is the lifting of warp threads running lengthwise of the loom and moving the shuttle that carries the weft or cross threads. If the warp threads are lifted selectively in a prescribed sequence, it is possible to weave a kind of damask pattern into the material. This had been done manually at considerable cost by silk weavers. It required as much as two weeks to set up a hand loom for weaving such material. The operation itself was a two-man job in which strings attached to groups of warp threads were drawn by hand at each pass of the shuttle. Jacquard succeeded in automatically controlling the lifting of warp threads by paste-board cards punched with holes. In his loom, rods are attached to groups of threads in the warp. These rods are then selectively lifted or not lifted at each pass of the shuttle by the absence or presence of holes in the punched cards. By feeding cards through the machine in a determined sequence, a complex pattern can be automatically woven into the fabric. In running the machine, the punched cards are strung end to end and passed by the rods in rapid sequence. Once a deck of cards has been punched for a particular pattern, it can be woven over and over in exact duplication. With the invention of Jacquard's loom, there were widespread strikes of silk weavers all over France. The price of tapestries tumbled and, interestingly enough, a new class of professionals was born. After an artist designed a fabric pattern, it was taken to one of these professionals who would translate the pattern into a proper set of punched cards for driving a Jacquard loom to weave it. These professionals were, we observe by hindsight, *loom programmers.*

There was a particularly famous tapestry of M. Jacquard himself hanging in drawing rooms all over Europe and England. It required no less than 24,000 punched cards for driving the loom to weave it. One of these tapestries found its way into the possession of Charles Babbage who saw in Jacquard's punched-card idea a means of controlling and storing numbers for his Analytical Engine.

## The Analytical Engine

Babbage conceived of the Analytical Engine as being composed of two main sections, namely, the *store* and the *mill.* The store consisted of mechanical counting registers not unlike those in modern desk calculators. The purpose of the store, as its name implies, was to hold numbers for use by the engine as its calculations proceeded. The mill was the central arithmetic unit in which the operations of addition, subtraction, multiplication, and division were performed. As Babbage planned it, orders to the mill for carrying out arithmetic steps in some predetermined sequence would be fed into the machine with Jacquard punched cards.

The Analytical Engine is shown schematically in [the following] figure. . . . It is notably similar to a modern automatic computer. Babbage further anticipated some important operational details worth remarking about. One of these is a facility called *branching*; this permits selection of future steps in a calculation sequence depending on the results of preceding steps. Babbage proposed to achieve this by advancing or reversing the punched cards a specified amount according to the sign of a number in one of the machine's registers. If the cards were moved ahead, some of the operations would be skipped; if moved back, some would be repeated. It was, as we now say, a "branch on sign," permitting

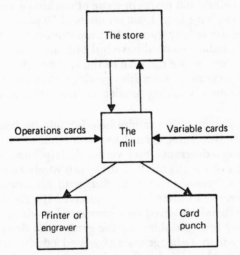

*Schematic Diagram of the Analytical Engine*
*Arrows Indicate Direction of Data Flow*

computationally dependent changes in subsequent steps to be selected by the Analytical Engine itself rather than by a human operator. To Babbage, this was equivalent to an exercise of judgment by the Analytical Engine, for it could choose one of two possible paths in a computing process without human intervention.

When we remember that the Analytical Engine could only have been entirely mechanical, that, for example, numbers punched in cards could only be mechanically transferred to registers in the mill and store, we can hardly be surprised that Babbage was hard pressed to bring his machine to reality. And, as in the case of his Difference Engine, Babbage thought big when selecting basic design parameters. The Analytical Engine was to have carried out its computation with a precision of 50 places; present-day machines rarely work to more than 8 or 10. If that weren't enough, Babbage even provided for hooking the registers of his machine end to end to allow 100 places or more of working accuracy! The store was to have held 1,000 numbers of 50 places each, a respectable size by any standard. It was not even remotely possible that Babbage could have built his automatic computer in its entirety before the turn of the century. But so detailed and comprehensive were his drawings, that after his death a scaled-down working model of the mill was actually constructed.

Today's generation cannot help but admire Babbage and his accomplishments, even if so much remained in the form of drawings, diagrams, and verbal descriptions. Automatic computers of the twentieth century can surely be considered Babbage's dreams come true. But, with his death in 1871, nearly forty years after he first conceived the Analytical Engine, the curtain lowered on a preview of modern automatic computing brought about by the genius and determination of a single man. Babbage once expressed a desire to exchange the balance of his life for three days five hundred years later. Perhaps, instead, he would have been just as pleased to see that the visions of his intellect, which could scarcely become real in his own century, would be a mighty force shaping the destiny of the next.

Babbage's ideas were essentially forgotten, and no further significant automatic-computing development took place until well into the twentieth century. But there was a continuing improvement in general machine technology. During Babbage's lifetime and shortly after, there were important inventions of electrical devices such as the telegraph in 1844 and the telephone in 1876. In 1884 the first key-driven adding machine appeared. Thus it was that two Americans,

Herman Hollerith and James Powers, were able to make very practical contributions toward the use of punched cards for the storing and processing of data. It had required seven years to complete the manual tabulation of the 1880 census. Hollerith, who with Powers worked for the United States Bureau of the Census, estimated that without some means of speeding the process, as long as twenty years might be required to tabulate the 1890 census. With a constantly growing United States population, there were grave doubts that any future census could be tabulated before the generation to which it applied had passed from the scene.

In the early 1880s, Hollerith and Powers began serious development of punched-card tabulating machines. By 1890, early models of their machines were in practical operation in the Census Bureau, enabling the 1890 census to be completely tabulated in less than three years. With all the success of Hollerith's machines, however, they were crude indeed compared with modern tabulating card equipment. Each hole in those early cards was punched separately by hand. To record the card, it was placed over a pool of mercury and a matrix of wires was lowered ends down over the card. Those wires passing through the holes made electrical contact with mercury to register on the dials of the tabulating machine. . . .

It was soon recognized that Hollerith's invention of punched-card tabulating equipment had more than ordinary implications. Applications for his machines were developed both in the United States and abroad. (Curiously enough, the most effective statistical uses of punched-card equipment were relatively slow to catch on in the United States. In several European countries, however, they were quickly adopted.) In 1890 the Franklin Institute awarded Hollerith the Elliott Cresson medal for the outstanding invention of that year. After obtaining patents on his machines, Hollerith formed a company to exploit further commercial applications of his ideas. In 1911 his company and two others merged to form the Computing-Tabulating-Recording Company, the name of which was changed in 1924 to International Business Machines Corporation.

Hollerith's colleague Powers also obtained patents for his version of mechanically actuated punched-card machines He also entered the commercial tabulating business. The Powers-Samas and Sperry Rand companies developed Powers' original patents. Hence, in the United States, we have two major styles in punched cards, a 90-column round-hole card produced by Sperry Rand and an 80-column rectangular-hole card produced by IBM and other companies. In France, the Compagnie Bull developed similar punched-card machines, using Norwegian patents. In the next few decades, electric accounting machines were developed, expanded, and improved rapidly.

The Social Security Act of 1935 had an accelerating effect on the growth of punched-card data processing in the United States. The social security system started the largest tabulating operation of all time. Also, the rising economic advantages of using punched-card tabulating equipment in the normal pursuits of business and industry helped motivate refinement and perfection of a wide variety of punched-card devices. Such development provided the technological spadework for the birth of automatic computers, which soon followed. Card punches, sorters, collators, calculating punches, and printers were being used to advantage in every conceivable industrial, business, and governmental application. Before much longer, almost every citizen would be on speaking terms with the ubiquitous punched card.

The widespread commercial use of punched-card tabulating equipment provided the broad technological base on which it became possible to build a working automatic computer. Also, the first three decades of the twentieth century saw the rapid practical development of the telephone, radio, and other electromechanical and electronic devices. All these developments were important precursors of practical high-speed computers. In a privately distributed paper dated November 4, 1937, Professor Howard Aiken of Harvard University proposed the construction of a fully automatic electromechanical computer. Many of this machine's basic components were standard items already widely used in electric accounting machines (EAM equipment). Aiken saw in commercially available punched-card machines the very feasibility of building his Mark I computer. Babbage had been forced to build his castle in the air; Aiken saw the real possibility of achieving his goal because he was in step with the prevailing technology of the late 1930s.

Actual work on the Mark I calculator was begun in 1939; it was completed in 1944 and was presented to Harvard University by the International Business Machines Corporation, the primary supporter of its development and construction. Mark I can be considered Babbage's dream at last come true, though elements of its basic design were quite different from the Analytical Engine. For one thing, Babbage could not have imagined the use of electrical components. For another, Aiken was not aware of Babbage's work and hence had to recover much of the same ground.

Mark I allowed for a precision of twenty-three places in its calculations. There were seventy-two arithmetic registers for adding and storing numbers and some sixty manual switches for setting constants into the machine. Whereas the multiplying and dividing units were physically separate from the seventy-two adding and storing registers, there was no sharp distinction between registers for arithmetic operations and those for storing numbers as in the case of the Analytical Engine. Input to the machine was either by setting manual switches or from standard punched cards. The output was either printed by electric typewriters or punched in cards. The card reading and the punching equipment were standard EAM items as were the arithmetic registers, relays, and other basic components.

Shortly after its completion, Mark I was put into operation twenty-four hours a day, seven days a week. In all, it was in productive operation for about fifteen years when it was retired in 1959. There is hardly a computation center in the United States without at least one set of tables calculated by Mark I. The machine is significant in several ways. It was the very first operational automatic computer and therefore dates the beginning of the modern computing era at about 1940. It focused attention on the importance of automatic computing as an essential tool in the further advance of science and technology. It was a very practical machine and, as a focal point of the vigorous Harvard Computation Laboratory under Aiken, continued to influence developments and interest in automatic computers for a number of years.

## THE VERSATILE MIDGETS [3]

The most exciting new development in electronics is the transistor, a tiny, simple device that can do the work of most vacuum tubes. Transistors are generally mounted in plastic or metal for easy handling, but the essential works of the smallest models are only one tenth of an inch long and fifteen-thousandths of an inch in diameter, hardly big enough to see without squinting. . . . Dr. A. E. Anderson of Bell Telephone Laboratories told a . . . meeting of the American Association of Aeronautical Engineers about the latest transistor progress. The airmen listened intently, because modern aircraft, especially military models, carry ever-increasing loads of vacuum tubes. Any chance of relief from this bulky burden is good news.

Transistors were invented . . . [in 1948] by a research group under Bell's Dr. William Shockley, and . . . [were then] developed for practical use by another team led by J. A. Morton. Their theory is complex in detail and full of difficult quantum mechanics, but their general principle is fairly simple.

### Between the Atoms

In an ordinary electron tube, electrons "boil" off a heated filament into a high vacuum. There, unhampered by clog-

[3] From *Time*. 59:57-9. F. 11, '52. Copyright Time Inc. 1952. Reprinted by permission.

ging air, they dance around obediently in response to electrical forces provided to act upon them. A transistor has no filament or vacuum, only a speck of hard germanium cut from a silvery crystal. But the mobile electrons are there, flashing through the empty channels between the ordered atoms of the crystal fragment.

In the outer shell of its atom, germanium has four electrons. If the crystal were absolutely pure germanium, each of these electrons would be bound by a neighboring atom. But if an occasional atom of an impurity such as phosphorus, which has five outer electrons, is built into the crystal, one of its electrons is not bound, and so is free to move around. If the impurity is an element with only three outer electrons, there is a "hole" into which electrons from germanium can move under certain conditions. Every time an electron moves into one hole, a new hole is left. When the holes move through the crystal, they produce the effect of electrons moving in the opposite direction.

### Points and Junctions

Some transistors (the "point contact" type) use only one kind of germanium with fine metal points pressing upon it. "Junction transistors" use both the germanium that has free electrons and germanium that has "holes." Both transistors act like electron tubes; they can turn alternating into direct current, amplify faint currents, generate musical tones, serve as relays; they even perform brilliantly as photoelectric cells, turning light into electricity.

All these chores are performed by the transistor with startling economy of materials and power. There is no glass envelope, as in an electron tube, and no complicated insides. The current price of germanium is more than $100 a pound, but so little is used that its cost is negligible.

The transistor's greatest advantage is its lack of a heated filament. Most of the currents that pulse through electronic apparatus are extremely small, but when they are amplified or relayed by a conventional vacuum tube, its filament consumes a full watt. It is the same, says Dr. Ralph Bown, vice president in charge of research at Bell Laboratories, as "sending a twelve-car freight train, locomotive and all, to carry a pound of butter." A transistor gets along with a millionth of a watt, not enough in most cases to make it faintly warm. The Bell men take a bit of blotting paper, chew it for a while, and wrap it moist around a twenty-five-cent piece. When wires are clipped to this combination, it makes a battery strong enough to work a transistor.

In such complicated devices as radars and computers, which use hundreds or even thousands of vacuum tubes, supplying the power is a serious problem. The heat developed by the tubes is even worse. To keep the temperature down, they must be well spaced and cooled by an air stream. Transistors cause no such problems; they can be "potted" in plastic and whole arrays put close together.

*Magic Trifle*

Bell laboratory has a two-stage transistor amplifier, complete with resistors and condensers, that is potted in a cylinder of plastic as big as a three-quarter-inch section cut from a fountain pen. When a faint voice current is fed to this trifle, it gives a signal loud enough to blast the eardrum. Scores of such amplifiers could be packed in a coffee can. One device at Bell has transistors that do the work of forty-four vacuum tubes. The whole thing is housed on a panel no bigger than the page of a novel.

The earliest transistors were skittish and unreliable. Now, says Bell, they are as reliable as conventional vacuum tubes, and much longer-lived. Some types are expected to work continuously for ninety thousand hours (ten years). . . .

Transistor enthusiasts speak of the future with electronic ecstasy. Replacing vacuum tubes, they say is not the whole story: transistors will be far more versatile than vacuum tubes. There may be transistor amplifiers in telephone receivers. Airplanes and guided missiles can carry electronic equipment that is now too heavy and fragile. Transistors will give a new impetus to development of electronic-control apparatus for automatic factories. Perhaps the most exciting possibility is in the rapidly growing field of electronic computers. Transistors can be built, theoretically, almost as small as the neurons (nerve cells) that serve as relays in the human brain, and they react several thousand times faster. A "brain" built with transistors instead of vacuum tubes might outcalculate a regiment of Einsteins and still fit in the room where Einstein does his thinking.

## MODERN COMPUTERS [4]

### The Electronic Computer

The era of the electronic computer came into being with ENIAC, Electronic Numerical Integrator and Computer, designed and built by Dr. John Mauchly and Dr. J. Presper Eckert.

Prior to ENIAC's "going on the air" (as computer men term the initial operation) in 1945, there were periods of dreaming, planning, hoping, being discouraged, and ultimately realizing success—steps that appear to accompany the emergence of most scientific products.

Mauchly, as a teacher, and Eckert, as a graduate student, met at the Moore School of Electrical Engineering of the University of Pennsylvania during World War II; each was involved in the activities of the Army's Aberdeen Proving Ground and felt deep concern about the inadequacy of the methods that then existed to supply urgently needed mathematical data for ballistic trajectories.

The two machines that were copies of Dr. Vannevar Bush's analog computer were being urgently employed in work for Aberdeen as were other pieces of equipment; there were many girls seated in cubicles throughout the University operating desk calculators—and still the output was totally inadequate. A real "breakthrough" type advance was needed.

[4] From *Computers: Their History, Present Applications and Future,"* by Shirley Thomas, author of a series of books on space. Holt. '65. p 61-73. Copyright © 1965 by Holt, Rinehart and Winston, Inc. Reprinted by permission.

Mauchly had prepared a proposal for an electronic computer and submitted it to the University. It became lost. At the urging of Dr. Herman Goldstein (then an Army liaison officer, now with IBM) Mauchly was able to reconstruct the proposal from shorthand notes, and Eckert added a considerable technical section; valuable help in the detailed planning was given by Dr. Arthur Burks. The proposal was submitted to Colonel Leslie E. Simon, at Aberdeen Proving Ground, and a contract was immediately forthcoming. Dr. Leland Cunningham (then at Aberdeen . . .) wrote the specifications for the machine.

The plan was for a very specialized computer for ballistics calculation. It was not designed as a general-purpose computer. To prove the design theory, Mauchly and Eckert first constructed and successfully tested 5 per cent of the machine. Then came the giant task of putting together the entire computer—with its 500,000 soldered joints, 18,000 tubes, 6,000 switches, and 5,000 terminals. Mauchly and Eckert, plus a team of ten engineers, labored two and one half years on this meticulous task, and during the construction they tripled the machine's function.

Whereas Mark I [see "Early History," in this section, above] could add two numbers in one third of a second, ENIAC could add numbers at the rate of five thousand per second. Gears were eliminated—the counting was performed by electronic pulses. This machine operated on the decimal system of numbers; the input was electromechanical, the output on punch cards. ENIAC had a master programmer, making it an automatically sequenced computer.

The project was classified as a wartime secret and all work was done behind locked and guarded doors. Those who did have clearance to enter the marvel under construction were amazed. Among the visitors was Dr. John von Neumann. This mathematical genius, as a consultant to Aberdeen, was able to suggest expanded use of the ENIAC. Von Neumann was also a consultant to Los Alamos on the Manhattan Project [for the development of an atomic bomb].

The initial test problem programmed into ENIAC that served as the machine's shakedown was one formulated by Dr. Nicholas Metropolis and Dr. Stanley Frankel; it related to the Manhattan Project. Though the machine performed as expected, Mauchly and Eckert kept expanding their thoughts, just as Babbage kept changing his Difference Engine during construction. Thus ENIAC, like a great proportion of machines ever constructed, was virtually obsolete even before it was completed. In a new and growing field, especially, the concepts expand at such a pace that it is almost impossible to keep abreast of technology.

ENIAC had gotten rid of the roll of paper tape that Mark I required and stored its instructions internally. However, the instructions had to be wired into the machines by means of hooking up appropriate circuits—a job that might involve hundreds of connections and require several days to perform. The means of short-cutting this tedious process was the invention of the stored program. Although there is still dispute as to who originated the stored-program idea, it is conclusive that the initial important paper on this and other modern computer concepts was the one written by Burks, Goldstein, and von Neumann on June 28, 1946, entitled *Preliminary Discussion of the Logical Design of an Electronic Computing Instrument.*

The first stored-program computer, EDSAC, went into operation at the University of Cambridge in 1949. EDVAC, a machine similar to EDSAC, begun by Mauchly and Eckert, was completed after they left the University of Pennsylvania and put into use at Aberdeen. The two men formed their own company, which was bought by Remington-Rand Corporation (later, Sperry Rand). Eckert . . . remained with . . . [Remington-Rand]; Mauchly left and formed Mauchly Associates, Inc.

Many of the design features proposed in the Burks, Goldstein, von Neumann paper were radical departures at that time; the soundness of them is indicated by the fact that not a dozen important differences exist between that machine and ones in use today. After World War II, von Neumann was relieved of some of his time-consuming consulting duties and was able to return to his post at the Institute for Advanced Study at Princeton. One of his first undertakings was the building of the computer described in the paper. Although the Army Ordnance Department financed the building of the machine, they requested in return only information in the form of reports and allowed the Institute to retain the machine. This computer is known variously as the von Neumann Machine, the Princeton Machine, or the IAS Machine.

This computer may be well appraised by the fact that it was copied, in principle if not in detail, in these and other machines: AVIDAC at Argonne National Laboratory, ORACLE at Oak Ridge, ILLIAC at the University of Illinois, ORDVAC at Aberdeen, MANIAC I at Los Alamos, SILLIAC at the University of Sydney, Australia, and JOHNNIAC at RAND. Also, the IBM-701 machine was patterned very much after the von Neumann Machine.

Comments Dr. Willis Ware, the RAND Corporation:

One commonly hears machines referred to as von Neumann-type machines. All the machines that we have today are essentially organized in a similar way. This has to do with the internal, logical structure, rather than the details of the individual electronic circuits.

The individual machines that sprung from the common ancestor had noteworthy characteristics of their own. MANIAC, for example, had a 1,024-word memory, which seemed practically infinite at a time when an 80-word memory was run-of-the-mill. This machine, in the opinion of scientists, was the means by which the United States was able to develop and test thermonuclear reaction (the principle of the H-bomb) prior to any other nation.

Computers have enabled scientists to play games—for very serious reasons. The fact that the machines can treat any number of samples in a statistical way enabled Dr. John von Neumann and Dr. Stanley Ulam to develop the Monte Carlo method which was used to solve an important problem in atomic energy—the distribution of neutrons radiating from an atomic pile outside the shielding. This information was vital to the safety of personnel working near an atomic pile.

England achieved two important computer firsts—the first workable electrostatic storage device, and the first commercially available electronic digital computer. But despite these early advances, the United States attained a leadership that has not been challenged.

Prior to 1947, the Army and the Manhattan District were powerful influences toward advancement of computer technology. Then the Office of Naval Research, ONR, formed a Computer Section with its Mathematics Branch under Dr. Mina Rees. Relates Dr. Joe [F. Joachim] Weyl [former head of the Mathematics and Physical Science Programs, ONR]:

> It became clear to some of us that something new was happening. What the United States Government was going to do in that area was something that would determine very profoundly and very essentially how the country was going to look across the board in its technology a decade hence. ONR was the first Government agency that had a clear recognition as to what the development of the computer was going to mean for science and technology—and acted on it.

ONR called together a steering committee, chaired by Dr. Rees and made up of representatives of various Government agencies, that did two principle things—surveyed ongoing programs to identify the gaps that existed in the overall effort, and then served as a collection point for funds from Government agencies to support further activity.

This led the Bureau of Standards into the computer-building business. The agency began a pilot project to construct at the Washington, D.C., location a computer named SEAC, Standards Eastern Automatic Computer. SEAC was the first U.S.-built stored-program computer. Then a second machine was begun for the Bureau's Institute of Numerical Analysis, located at the University of California, Los Angeles. This was called SWAC, Standards Western Automatic Computer. (SWAC later was taken out from under the Bureau of

Standards and made a research project of UCLA because those in Government who protect small business felt that it was competitive.)

Both SEAC and SWAC were under Air Force financial sponsorship; the aim in undertaking them was to build "state of the art" computers—ones based on the level of technological development that then existed—and to put them into operation within two years. In that way, it was hoped to gain experience in the operation of installations before the really big and fast machines were ready. However, computer-building was new, strange, and complicated. As it turned out, SEAC and SWAC were not ready [very] long before such elaborate machines as UNIVAC I. (This inability to accurately estimate a completion date is expressed in what has been termed the "von Neumann constant"—at any given time, the completion seems about one year away.)

The steering committee spearheaded by ONR reached another salient conclusion—that in all the concentration on *machines, people* were being forgotten. No group was giving thought to the establishment of a systematic plan to train computer personnel, though it was already clear that increasing numbers of complex machines would make sizable manpower demands.

ONR pioneered the development of training programs that were particularly oriented toward supplying the needs of the Department of Defense; these programs started the pattern that is now followed by computer manufacturers. ONR further succeeded in establishing computer mathematics as an important new field and in gaining the interest and participation of leading mathematicians.

A complicated mathematical model—which involved the simulation of high performance trainer aircraft—led to the concept of a very fast machine, Whirlwind II. This ranks as one of ONR's most important early projects; it was developed by the Digital Computer Laboratory of MIT. The name described its primary characteristics—a target speed of fifty thousand operations per second. Whereas the von Neu-

mann machine operated at a 1-megacycle rate, Whirlwind
ran at 4. However, in order to do this it sacrificed accuracy,
having a register size of only 16 bits as compared with the
40 bits of the von Neumann machine.

As the design developed, great controversy arose and it
was said that Whirlwind would never work. The pessimists
were almost right. During the first period of Whirlwind's
operation, it chalked up a calamitous record of failure—
whereas the slower-but-surer Mark I machine, with its relay
operation, kept plugging away.

It is to the very great credit of those responsible that
Whirlwind eventually achieved a reliability record of 85
per cent. This was to a large measure achieved by the joint
MIT-Sylvania development of the 7AK7 tube, the first one
made especially for use in computers. These tubes attained
an average life of 500,000 hours.

As an added form of insurance when something did go
amiss with one particularly weak point, Whirlwind was programmed to instruct the operator how to make repairs! This
imaginative maintenance program typed out a list of instructions. The final step in the repair was to go down the hall,
around the corridor, down a flight of stairs, and make a critical voltage check. The machine timed the operator's activities; if the signal to start came too soon, Whirlwind would
query, "Are you sure you checked the voltage?" The operator
had to reply, "Yes," before the machine would start.

### Magnetic Core Memory

A giant technological stride was taken with the magnetic
core memory, which was the second type installed in Whirlwind. (The original one was an electrostatic memory.) The
magnetic core memory was the great contribution by Dr.
Jay W. Forrester, and its significance is noted by Dr. Frederick Frick, "Insofar as any one development or invention
has made the modern computer possible, it has been the
memory core."

The ideal utilization for Whirlwind presented itself in the summer of 1951 when it became apparent we needed to guard our nation against surprise air attack. The information that came off a major air surveillance radar was fed into the Whirlwind by means of a data link, and it was found that the computer could very effectively sort out that data, and relate the radar returns to the right target tracks! As Dr. Joe Weyl so eloquently phrases it:

> Though the development of Whirlwind was a checkered one, it stepped on the stage of world history during a very important period and vindicated all the cost and trouble of the entire project.

The final achievement of this MIT computer lent special meaning to a statement that Dr. Jay W. Forrester had made in an address years earlier:

> I believe that if a high-speed computer . . . were sitting here today, it would be nearly two years before the machine were in effective and efficient operation. One would be caught totally unprepared for feeding to this equipment problems at its high acceptance rate. On the other hand, this represents but one half of a vicious circle in which an adequate national interest in computer training cannot be developed until the equipment is actually available.

### The "Real-Time" Computer

To make available a system for the next requirements of air defense was one of the most challenging problems that has ever faced computer scientists. In 1952, Lincoln Laboratory of MIT was established under Air Force support with the mission to develop SAGE, Semi-Automatic Ground Environment. The parameters were beyond experience, beyond the technology—seemingly beyond reason. Specifications called for speeds that were almost instantaneous, sizes that were almost infinite. Our defense demanded the development of such equipment. To preserve freedom, it was essential that our nation be ringed with radar's searching eyes, that forces stand ready to intercept, and that instantaneous detection and reaction become our way of life. Admittedly beyond the capability of men alone, such aims could be realized only with the augmentation of machines.

By means of appropriately placed computer systems, SAGE has to perform "real-time" (as it happens) interpretation of information gathered by radar. Sequentially, it has to identify as friendly or unknown every aircraft in the skies above our nation and Canada, and to furnish information on its location, speed, specifications. If the aircraft remains unknown, the computer must next determine and designate which of our ADC [Air Defense Command] aircraft are to "scramble" and intercept and, immediately, it computes the trajectory for missiles that are standing ready. Though we now have been so surfeited with technological achievements that such functions as these seem little more than routine, SAGE must be considered in the context of its planning phase a decade ago. These were giant goals.

In addition to the innovation of a real-time operation, there was another—the use of computers for processing information. The functions of the SAGE operation are only in small part mathematical—largely they are a supercolossal bookkeeping system. Computers have to store data, retrieve data, file data, check data, up-date data, rearrange data. This kind of function is now an accepted application of the equipment, but it was a revolutionary use in that day.

For the handling of such masses of information, machines far larger than any then known were required. An entire new elephantine breed of equipment came into being, and has since thrived on a diversity of applications. Lincoln Laboratory brought in IBM as contractor, and much of the equipment development was a joint effort. This became something of a turning point for that company; it put them in the large-scale computer business.

In all ways, SAGE evolvement gave explosive acceleration to the technological state of the art and was a milestone for military applications. It is the closed loop, the total system. Yet, equipment, *hardware*, is but half the requirement. It cannot perform without its partner, the programming, or *software*. Some of the first programming was done at Lincoln

Laboratory, but the task became too vast, and was assigned to the RAND Corporation.

This organization, known as a think factory, was established in 1946 largely to give guidance to the Air Force on long-range research and development programs. Dr. Cecil Hastings, Jr., the man at RAND who pioneered computing at an early date, rented IBM accounting equipment. (He selected an 016 key punch, feeling a larger machine was ruled out because of its high rental—$30 per month!) Later, when RAND got news of the machine that von Neumann had under construction, they set out to build a copy of it; they named it, in tribute to its designer, JOHNNIAC.

But even this machine was not capable of solving one giant problem that faced the scientists at RAND, so on one of von Neumann's visits to that organization, they solicited his help in designing a new supercomputer. He asked just what the problem was that had them stumped. The array of scientists began describing it. For the next two hours with the use of formulas, diagrams, and tables, they conveyed the extent of it. Then the group waited for the genius to describe the kind of computer that would solve the problem. He stared blankly into space, scribbled for a moment, then said, "Here is your answer. You won't need a new computer."

The problem assigned to RAND in programming SAGE was almost as complex, and far more time-consuming. So immense did the undertaking grow that the section of RAND devoted to it became like the tail wagging the dog. A change was clearly indicated. This section "spun off" and became a new organization, SDC, Systems Development Corporation. Several hundred people at SDC worked several years on two aspects of SAGE—writing the program for the computers, and training people to operate the system.

But modifications alone could not keep pace with the war-making potential of this era. Whereas nuclear bombs delivered by long-range bombers had been the concern of SAGE, a new threat arose—bombs delivered by intercontinental ballistic missiles that travel many times the speed of aircraft. BMEWS, Ballistic Missile Early Warning System, a billion-dollar-plus installation, was begun in 1959. The first site went into operation at Thule, Greenland, two years later.

BMEWS is the largest integrated electronics system ever developed, and consists of three basic elements—extremely powerful radar, extremely efficient computers to sort out and reduce the data from the radar, and extremely reliable communications equipment to transmit the data to NORAD, North American Air Defense Headquarters, at Colorado Springs. The reliability requirements on the entire system were incredibly high—99.99 per cent.

BMEWS was to warn of any mass missile attack over the northern hemisphere. Soon after it went into operation, the radars spotted a mass of targets over the horizon, the computers reduced the data, and headquarters went on red alert. But, fortunately, there is always the top-level judgment of men to interpret what equipment tells them. Instead of immediately launching a retaliatory attack, the commanders took a second look at what was happening—and found that the mass appearing over the horizon was only the rising moon!

From the development of ballistic missiles came orbital capability. The military must monitor space as closely as it does air, and computers aid men in the vigil. To fulfill the needs presented by these and hundreds of other requirements, there is an array of equipment that is wondrous in its capability and versatility. Today's production output becomes the more remarkable when it is remembered that the first years of the computer effort manifested one-of-a-kind, made-by-hand machines. They were indeed the progeny of their designers, with individual names and distinct personalities. Sometimes they performed in ways that delighted, and other times they were recalcitrant children, balking in such a frustrating manner that even a usually well-controlled lady programmer, Mrs. Ruth Horgan, once kicked a computer!

This equipment became very personal because it had to be "raised." Computers know only what they are told—and told in absolutely painful detail. Then, with the introduction of compilers, some of the programming burden could be placed upon the machine. With the maturing of the computer, not only was the individuality of each machine submerged, but, also, the era of the single inventor vanished. Complexity demanded teams, not individual men, to do the design work.

In those years of eager interest and consecration to the cause of computing, the scattered but keenly sympathetic group of pioneers spread word of their activities by means of what was one of the first publications in the computing field, *Computing News*. This was edited by Fred Gruenberger when he was an instructor at the University of Wisconsin. The means of subscribing was most novel—at the first of the year, each subscriber simply mailed to Gruenberger twelve stamped, self-addressed envelopes.

Even at this time it is difficult to draw a line of demarcation where commercial production tipped the balance over pioneering creativity. Some will say that computers came of age with the CPC, Card Programmed Calculator; it was the first to be widely used by engineers. The credit for development is shared by IBM and Northrop Corporation. A true pioneer, Northrop farsightedly formed a digital computer group in 1946, and ordered the BINAC machine from Eckert and Mauchly the following year. Other aircraft companies were also avant-garde in the stampede toward data processing.

The beginning of the electronic computer industry dates from UNIVAC [Remington-Rand]. The first machine was delivered to the Bureau of the Census early in 1951, the second to the Air Force later that year, and the third in 1952 to the Army Map Service. (The Government got these first machines at a bargain price—about $250,000. Later models sold for about $1.5 million.) General Electric Company initiated the business use of UNIVAC machines, followed by Metropolitan

Life Insurance Company. Despite these major sales, there was no widespread conviction that a real market for computers existed.

A few smaller groups, with more faith than financing, endeavored to get a foothold in the future. Though they fell by the wayside, perhaps it was their rustlings that prompted IBM to investigate further. Still playing it safe, the company approached the defense contractors and proposed a machine called the Defense Calculator—subsequently designated IBM-701. IBM decided that if they could secure thirteen firm contracts, they would produce the machine. They exceeded their goal, for they got contracts to build nineteen machines. With that, a great leap was taken in the industrial use of computers. Further, it generated momentum within IBM. The first IBM-701 was delivered in the spring of 1953. A year later, they brought out a computer suitable for either scientific or business use that became the workhorse of industry, the IBM-650; nearly two thousand of these machines were eventually produced.

As technological advances were made, the need for interchange of information became more imperative. As an outgrowth of a meeting at the Harvard Computation Laboratory in 1947, the Association for Computing Machinery was formed.

But of all these gatherings, none had more far-reaching implications than a meeting late in 1954 of a group of Southern California users of IBM-701's. The meeting came about largely through the efforts of R. Blair Smith, IBM; he perceived, as did others, that the amount of redundant effort expended on systems and programs for the IBM-701 had been horrendous—usually in excess of a year's rental for the machine. Jack Strong and Frank Wagner, both with North American Aviation, Inc., at that time, suggested a cooperative effort be undertaken toward devising a better coding system for the IBM-701's.

PACT, the coding system they subsequently devised, was little used, because at just about that same time IBM brought out a computer language known as SPEEDCODE. But the spirit of this joint effort of the IBM-701 users ripened into one of the most unusual features of the entire computer picture, *cooperative user groups*.

George Bynum, Corporate Director of Data Processing, North American Aviation, Inc., vividly recalls the early struggles. He says the inspiration for user groups can be summed up in one word: "Desperation. At that time, everyone had a high degree of ignorance about use of computers. We wanted company in our misery."

SHARE, the first of the groups, was made up of those who acquired IBM-704's. The aim of the organization, quite simply, was to try to eliminate redundant effort among its members with regard to use of the computers.

The user groups have been a remarkable effort, for seldom, if ever, has there been demonstrated such cooperation between different organizations. The mutual effort for the mutual good proved so effective that each major computer system now has its own user group. They are known by intriguing names such as POOL, GUIDE, USE, DUE, and TUG.

Another major invention ushered in the present era of computers. In 1952, Bell Laboratories announced that three of their scientists had created the transistor, a device with boundless applications. [See preceding selection, "The Versatile Midgets."] Its benefits to computer design were immediately obvious: The transistor eliminates the vacuum tube, reduces size by an order of magnitude, adds greatly to reliability, and slashes cost. Hardly could more be asked of one tiny device.

The face of history is ever changing. The first business machines had used notched wheels for counting. Wheels gave way to vacuum tubes. Tubes were replaced by transistors. And next, transistors are giving way to . . . . But that is another chapter.

We have reached the point where the present is a bridge across the growing edge of progress leading us from the past to the future.

# IV. THE IMMEDIATE IMPACT

## EDITOR'S INTRODUCTION

Though the computer revolution is still in its infancy its impact has already been enormous. On the one hand the machines have made possible such incredible feats as man's first flight to the moon. On the other, they have stirred bitterness and anxiety over the prospect that they may do away with jobs that men now have.

The first selection in this section is a poignant portrait of the human toll that computer-aided automation can take. Indeed, the writer notes that the greatest fear among factory workers is that at any time a computer-run machine might simply replace them at their job.

The next article reports that a study by a presidential commission found that, in the aggregate, the job displacement automation causes is not unmanageable. It suggests that while some jobs are eliminated many others are created—a conclusion well-supported by the low unemployment rates of the late 1960s.

But the impact of increasingly sophisticated technology and automation is not uniform. The less educated find that with each forward step they become less and less useful to society. The third selection focuses on the joint government and business effort to train hard-core unemployed so that they can become productive workers. This kind of large-scale training is a brand new phenomenon. One of the things it suggests is that such special training may eventually be the order of the day for a great many workers, not just the hard-core unemployed, as our computer-aided technology surges ahead.

Just how big some of these forward steps have been is almost impossible to document. But one of the most dramatic is man's first moon landing. In the next selection a ranking officer of the United States space program explains how computers made an otherwise impossible trip feasible.

The two articles that follow give us a clue as to how pervasive the impact has been. The first discusses the advent of the minicomputer; the second relates how so much of our financial dealing has been put on computers that it has even bred a special group of thieves who specialize in using their knowledge of computers to swindle people.

The brief final selection notes that the growing explosion of knowledge that the computer is helping to generate in the United States is creating concern among other nations. It is clear that prosperity and technological knowledge are linked very closely. What bothers other nations is that our fund of that knowledge is growing so quickly that it is creating a "knowledge gap" between this nation and others and, consequently, also a widening between the standard of living enjoyed here and that of many other nations.

## THE HARDEST BLOW [1]

When Albert MacGinn left his house that morning in March of 1963, he had no way of knowing that by nightfall his private world would lie in ruins.

An erect and pink-cheeked man with steel-rimmed glasses, Al MacGinn was the living model of American prosperity, a skilled worker in a nation whose farms and factories were producing at fabulous rates and employing more people than ever before. After twenty-four years in a growing industry in St. Paul, Minnesota, he was getting the top wage of $3.55 an hour. When he left for work it was from his own single-family stucco house with a new roof and a modernized kitchen. He drove to work and returned in his own automobile. Al MacGinn had played it by the rule book. He worked hard

[1] From "I'm Out of a Job, I'm All Through," by Ben Bagdikian, free-lance writer. *Saturday Evening Post*. 238:32-6+. D. 18, '65. Copyright © 1966 by Ben Bagdikian. Reprinted by permission of The Sterling Lord Agency.

and he did well. So when he returned home in the gathering dusk of that March evening, his fate seemed so improbable that he found it hard to tell his wife the truth.

"Kathy, I'm out of a job. I'm all through."

She stood motionless for a long moment, then said quietly, "Al, we'll get by. You'll be at work again next week."

At supper he announced the news to their five children. They fell into stunned silence. The oldest son, the one planning to start college the next year, said, "Dad, you're the best in the business. The other plants will be calling you up." Everyone agreed. Spirits rose, and the meal ended with something like gaiety.

They all were wrong. Al MacGinn has never again worked at his trade. After bitter months of unemployment he finally got the job he still has today—scrubbing toilets on the night shift of a nearby factory.

But Al MacGinn was luckier than many. According to government surveys, three million Americans can find no work, though they look for it, and more than two million who want full-time work can get only part-time. Even these official statistics are rosier than reality. They do not tell of skilled men in midcareer who can get only menial jobs. Nor do they show the more than one million "hidden unemployed" who are uncounted because they have finally given up looking for work. These and others are ignored in the surveys.

For all these millions and their families the richness of the American economy is worse than meaningless. It not only leaves them without work but surrounds them with the sight and sound of prosperity, increasing their isolation and despair. In a depression, unemployment is at least normal. In boom times, it makes the jobless man an outcast among his neighbors. While almost everyone around him is succeeding, he is failing, often for reasons that are a mystery to him.

Only a person who has experienced the stunning blow of the old job suddenly destroyed can appreciate its force.

It is a shock so profound that it damages the victim's will to recover. Sometimes the human destruction is apparent and measurable. Within a few years after the 1954 closing of the Hudson Motor Car Company, fifteen auto workers committed suicide and the marriages of more than three hundred workers broke up. . . . [In 1964] when the Government announced that the Brooklyn Navy Yard would close in June 1966, on-the-job injuries increased 50 per cent, off-the-job accidents went up, and the death rate rose.

Most of the suffering, however, is private and unrecorded. Recently this reporter talked with perhaps 150 men who have lost their jobs, and their reactions dramatize their experience.

A fifty-nine-year-old millwright:

I was sick two or three weeks. Couldn't eat, couldn't sleep. In forty years I had only seven days lost time, but they announce over the PA, "That's all."

A forty-five-year-old auto worker:

The day they announced the closing, the guy next to me, he just went blank. He'd worked there thirty, thirty-five years. His wife was an invalid with arthritis, and he had a son and a daughter still in college. He just stood there like someone hit him with a hammer. I practically had to lead him out to the car.

A forty-nine-year-old auto worker:

I saw men cry I'd never seen shed a tear. Grown men standing there with tears coming down their cheeks. Remember, these are tough bastards who'd been through the depression and the war, some of them two wars.

These reactions conflict with the stereotype of the American workingman as a lazy and cynical rate jockey. They also reflect the shock of the suddenly jobless man as he discovers how quickly an interruption in wages can destroy normal family life in the city. Especially for the older worker they suggest that the death of a job disrupts a deep rhythm in life and implies the death of the man.

The unemployment of 1965 is not the massive idleness of the great Depression, of course, or even of the recessions of the 1950s. But neither is it a small or a transient problem. It is a faulty part in the economic machine, a malfunctioning gear in danger of mangling itself and crippling the rest of the engine. Already the harsh sounds of this flawed machine have been heard: gunfire from bitter coal miners in Kentucky, the roar of flames during the Watts rebellion in Los Angeles, the shouts of rioters in Harlem and Rochester, New York, and Springfield, Massachusetts.

Despite periodic panics and depressions during the last one hundred years, the country has never produced a durable solution for unemployment. In the great Depression, joblessness reached at least 25 per cent. By the end of the 1930s it was still an intolerable 15 per cent. (Economists consider 3 per cent tolerable because at any given moment about 3 per cent of the work force is temporarily out of work—men changing jobs, for example, or young people not yet hired for the first time.)

Pearl Harbor brought the grisly full employment of war, when part of the population works at destruction and the remainder supplies the destroyers. The postwar demand for scarce goods kept men busy, but by 1949 the unemployment rate was up to 5.9 per cent. The Korean War made jobs, but after that the rate went back to 5 per cent.

. . . [The 1965] rate promises to be about 4.5 per cent, an improvement due in part to the economic expansion for the war in Vietnam. But much of the change occurred because many of the jobless were soaked up by activities like the antipoverty program and were counted as employed. Yet most of these people must emerge from the special programs to look for work. If they were now counted as unemployed, the total count of jobless would be over three million.

Through all the subtleties of statistics it is clear that the normal labor market does not provide a job for every American who needs one.

It is impossible to understand the impact of unemployment by dwelling on the national average of 4.5 or 5, or 7 per cent. The idle are not distributed evenly through the nation but concentrated in bitter masses: among all Negroes, 10 per cent; among all the young, 16 per cent; among young Negroes, 26 per cent. While most of the population enjoys employment and prosperity, there are masses of Americans who, for all intents and purposes, still live in the depths of the depression.

The irony is that those who prosper can thank science, and so can the unemployed. The application of the scientific method to the growing of food and making of goods has produced enormous wealth that has rapidly raised the standard of living. More goods at cheaper prices are available to a larger proportion of the population than ever before in history.

But the same scientific method has denied this standard of living to a portion of the population. It permits new machines to produce goods with fewer human beings at the same time that it has vastly increased the human life-span. Since 1900 our total population increased two and one half times, and the new standard of living has added an average of twenty years to the life-span of each of these new Americans. But the new machines don't need all the new Americans.

The most awesome instrument of change for the working-man in our time is the computer that runs an automatic machine. Two years ago, for example, an electronics company bought two computerized devices that automatically wired circuits for radios. The company was able to reduce the circuit-wiring work force from seventeen men to three. Today the company has doubled its production with the same two machines, which now do the work formerly done by thirty-five men. But it still requires only three human beings.

The rise of automation has been so swift that no one knows how many more human jobs it will eliminate. In 1954 there were fewer than 400 computers in use. Today there are more than 25,000, and most of their owners can't find enough work for them to do. So it is impossible to predict how much of the nation's work could be done by present computers, not to mention the 8,000 computers on order. And there are still other kinds of laborsaving changes. With machinery one man can lay down weed-killing chemicals that will do the work that it would take 360 human weeders to do. It is irrational to expect such change to slacken.

The new methods have also changed the occupations of men, changed them so fast that unemployment exists partly because men's experience and schooling, even though it may be better than that of their fathers, is not good enough to keep up with the revolution in technology. The latest edition of the *Dictionary of Occupations* lists 23,000 different jobs in the United States; 6,000 of them did not even exist ten years ago.

The drift in modern human labor is away from the simple workman to the man who thinks and adapts. Aristotle once said that the educated are as different from the uneducated "as the living are from the dead." A modern Aristotelian who happened to be a Chicago slum kid put it to me, "Man, you got no education, you're dead." In 1950 if a person had gone no further than fourth grade, the odds of his being unemployed were one in twelve. Today they are one in six.

Let no white-collar worker think he is immune. Already typists, filing clerks, bookkeepers and even management men who evaluate inventory and place orders are being replaced by computerized machines. In 1960 the *Harvard Business Review* said that "for every five office jobs eliminated, only one is created by automation."

Yet optimists continue to comfort themselves that the new machines *ultimately* will make enough jobs for all. They point reassuringly to earlier work changes seemingly as drastic as modern ones—to the introduction of knitting machines into textile manufacturing, for example, during the Industrial Revolution; *ultimately,* they say, those new machines expanded employment. They overlook two things. First, the early changes brought massive suffering, with riots and revolutions and wars. Second, these changes came to societies still largely wedded to the land, and the land guaranteed many of the unemployed a source of food and a place to live.

Today the average worker is a city dweller who has many fixed expenses. Even if it were true that machines eventually produce enough jobs—and it has not been true for a long time—his family needs food, shelter, medicine and a place in the working world not ultimately but now.

Fifty years ago, when the automobile put the blacksmith out of business, the blacksmith left his trade by ones and twos and threes in otherwise healthy towns. Today it is 79,000 jobs lost on the East Side of Detroit in ten years, or 12,000 lost in San Diego in two years, or 7,000 lost in South Bend in one year. When this happens, it leaves masses of men jammed explosively together in misery, and it cripples their community.

Industry is organized in gigantic units, partly because such super-units can best afford maximum automation. The giant corporation is not like the local industry a century ago, limited to just one town. Corporations today span the entire country, whole continents, the globe; they move factories thousands of miles, quickly abolish old products and invent new ones and change their work force in multiples of thousands of men.

The new machines affect the life of the community in a new way. In 1913 the equivalent of automation was Henry Ford's assembly line, and in ten years Ford increased production of his cars from 203,000 to 2 million. This vast jump was possible because, when he started, only one American in one hundred owned a car, and despite the new efficiency the market rose so much that he increased his work force from 14,000 to 128,000. But in 1950, when Detroit started automating, one American in four already had a car. Detroit was not able to increase production 1,000 per cent, as Henry Ford had, but only 12 per cent. The chief effect of its automation was to increase profits and reduce employment 6 per cent.

The giant units, the swiftness of change, the packing of people in cities—this all means that the whole system is sensitive to shock as never before. A cutback in automobile production shakes the entire economy and may determine whether Mrs. Albert MacGinn in St. Paul will buy a new refrigerator, how much interest she will pay on a loan, or if her husband will find a job.

## THE PROBLEM CAN BE SOLVED [2]

A presidential commission on automation has unanimously agreed to a report that finds technological change presents no basic threat to employment that cannot be overcome by vigorous fiscal policies to spur economic growth.

Authoritative sources said today that all members of the fourteen-man commission voted yesterday to adopt a report in which this was the central theme after changes had been made to meet the objections of three labor members, who had planned to file a dissenting minority report.

A strong drive was made to accommodate the views of the labor members with those of the members of the business and academic communities who make up the balance of the commission. This was done to prevent a minority dissent that would have damaged the report's influence. The central theme of the report remained intact, despite the changes.

Sources said that the basic finding was that the rate of technological change had been increasing but the rate of increase has not broken the continuity of the past, and that it is manageable if an expansionary fiscal policy is pursued.

### Combinations of Programs

This finding is coupled with recommendations that the nation seek to meet the challenge of advancing technology with a far-ranging combination of public and private programs. It favors a substantial increase in Government spend-

[2] From "Automation Panel Agrees on Report," by David R. Jones, staff reporter. New York *Times*. p 15. Ja. 24, '66. © 1966 by The New York Times Company. Reprinted by permission.

ing, Government employment for all those unable to find jobs, and some tax cuts.

The report also favors a negative income tax or some other income-maintenance device to replace or supplement welfare programs by paying families whose breadwinners are unemployable.

The report also proposes fourteen years of free public schooling, a commitment to provide every qualified person with a college education, a new "commission on national goals" to help the nation benefit fully from changing technology, and other steps.

The report has been prepared by the National Commission on Technology, Automation, and Economic Progress, set up seventeen months ago by Congress at the request of President Johnson.

The commission was directed to study the impact of technological change, define areas of human needs that would benefit from application of the technology, and assess means of channeling the technology. . . .

The union members believed that the tone of the earlier drafts had been too sanguine, and feared that the report would lull the public into complacency about automation.

The report originally stated that technological change had been a notable feature of the national economy for decades, and that the rate of change had been moderately accelerating. It then went on to say that this change had produced dislocations that had to be offset by vigorous economic policies.

### Vigorous Steps to Adjust Needed

The final report . . . [retains] the theme that technological change is manageable, sources said, but it will merely state that the rate is increasing without specifying at what pace.

The final report . . . [lays] more emphasis on the need to take vigorous steps to adjust to this change, sources said.

The commission at . . . [a] meeting deleted the original suggestion that seniority provisions in labor agreements often lead to racial discrimination and interfere with the job mobility needed to adjust to changing technology.

The union members had considered this an attack on the seniority system.

At an earlier meeting, the commission went a long way toward accommodating the views of the labor members by eliminating the idea that this was not the time to reduce the hours of work because the nation needed its full productive power.

This was a major victory for the union members who favor a shorter work week, and probably held the key to their final endorsement of the report.


## HARBINGER OF THE FUTURE? [3]

Lockheed Aircraft Corporation, one of the first major companies to recruit and train workers among those formerly considered unemployable, is taking a hard look at results.

Its decision: Problems are many and solutions not easy to come by. But the unskilled, unschooled "hard core" can be trained to do a job that in most cases is as good as that done by a normally hired employee.

Lockheed regards its pilot programs in hard-core training as a success and is expanding them.

The company does not minimize the problems involved. Its officials do not feel that they have the total answer. But lessons learned at Lockheed could make the job easier for other members of the National Alliance of Businessmen, which, with Government encouragement, has pledged to find jobs for 100,000 unemployed by July 1969, and 500,000 by July 1971.

Lockheed has programs of varying degree in 10 of the 50 cities cooperating in the Federal effort, but the company's first formal venture into hard-core training is at the subsidiary Lockheed-Georgia Company in Marietta, Georgia, and

[3] From "Training the Unemployables." Reprinted from *U.S. News & World Report.* 65:54-7. Jl. 1, '68.

the Lockheed Missiles & Space Company in Sunnyvale, near San Francisco.

## Requirements in Reverse

Because it wants only the hardest of the hard core in the pilot programs, Lockheed has set up five negative standards and requires prospective trainees to meet four of them.

To qualify, a trainee has to be a school dropout, unemployed, with no consistent record of work of any kind and have an annual family income of $3,000 or below.

Among recruits, a certain percentage must have arrest records, and a heavy proportion are to be drawn from minorities. Most are Negro.

According to a Lockheed official:

> We intended to make sure they were the hard core. Some men were weeded out at the start because they didn't meet the low standards. There were some who didn't get jobs because they were too well qualified.

At Lockheed-Georgia, ninety-eight trainees entered the first twelve-week program. They received $20 to $30 a week, plus $5 per dependent and an allowance to cover transportation.

Eighteen quit before training ended, and ten were fired, in most cases because they failed to attend classes regularly or were habitually late. Of the sixty-one who finished training, Lockheed hired forty-three. Other companies hired most of the remainder. Of the forty-three who stayed with Lockheed, only three were fired later for poor attendance.

According to Lockheed, most of the men who dropped out did so because they found they could not live on the small allowance that was paid them during training.

## Allowance vs. Payroll

At the Sunnyvale plant, 108 trainees were enrolled in two programs. In one, they received a training allowance. In the other, they went directly on the company payroll at $2.40 to $2.80 an hour. Five quit, four were fired and one was ar-

rested and convicted of a felony. None was fired for inability
to do the work.

A Lockheed official says this:

> A comparison study with a group of fifty new employees who
> met traditional hiring standards and entered the same occupations
> during the period indicated no difference between the hard-core
> and traditional trainees on rating of quality and quantity of work.

James D. Hodgson, Lockheed's vice president for industrial relations at corporate headquarters . . . in Burbank
[California], originated the company's programs. He says:

> There are certain criteria. Has it hurt production? Has it in-
> creased employee turnover? The answer to both is no. Has it
> caused disaffection among other employes? Not to any significant
> extent.
> So we think from a company standpoint, it is a success. From
> the standpoint of the nation, people who have been thought un-
> employable have proved to be employable.

E. G. Mattison, corporate personnel director, agrees. He
says:

> We used to wonder if the hard-core men could be trained. The
> answer is: They sure can. They can become as competent as regu-
> larly hired employees, some even better.

Lockheed-Georgia officials say they have had two job
offers from other companies for every man trained in the program whom Lockheed cannot put on its own payroll.

Encouraged by results, Lockheed this year is doubling
the size of the project at Sunnyvale and is enlarging the
Georgia program.

## COMPUTERS AND THE MOON SHOT [4]

If I had to single out the piece of equipment that, more
than any other, has allowed us to go from earth-orbit Mer-

[4] From "Computers and Controllers," by Christopher C. Kraft, Jr., director
of flight operations at NASA's Manned Spacecraft Center in Houston, Tex.
New York *Times.* p 36. Jl. 17, '69. © 1969 by The New York Times Company.
Reprinted by permission.

cury flights to Apollo lunar trips in just over seven years, it would be the high-speed computer.

On Apollo, we have begun to use computers, literally, by the hundreds.

They are used, first of all, to check out the space vehicle before launching. And then they help to carry out the launching itself.

During flight, miniaturized computers jammed with more data than the full-sized, on-the-ground computers, that handled entire Mercury flights perform incredibly complex jobs. They keep track of speed and position; calculate needed changes in flight path; watch for malfunctions; and display data on "cockpit" panels.

But it is in the operation of the worldwide network supporting each Apollo flight that the full scope of what the computer contributes to a lunar voyage can best be appreciated.

The network consists of seventeen ground stations, four instrumented ships and half a dozen or more instrumented planes. The role of the network is to keep the flight-control center at Houston in almost instantaneous contact with the spacecraft with just a few exceptions. These come during the brief periods that the spacecraft is between network stations on initial earth orbits, and for about forty-five minutes of each lunar orbit, when the crew modules are behind the moon.

Even for sophisticated engineers, it is hard to comprehend fully what a fantastic advance this Apollo network represents.

In the Mercury program, we had relatively simple needs. Our chief concern right after launching was to determine whether the spacecraft had been rocketed into a satisfactory earth orbit and, if not, what actions we should take to accomplish a safe recovery. Once the capsule was in a proper orbit, the only maneuver that could change the flight path was the retro-fire that would slow the vehicle to bring it out of orbit and down to a safe landing.

The problems of assessing whether the initial orbit was satisfactory, and of assuring safe recovery, seemed monumental. But comparing them with the problems involved in carrying out the many combinations of maneuvers required on a lunar mission is like comparing simple addition to the most complex mathematical equation.

The communications that initially tied together the worldwide Mercury network consisted mainly of messages sent over low-speed teletype equipment. But that would not permit any direct voice contact between the flight controller at what was then called Cape Canaveral and the orbiting astronaut, except when the Mercury passed within range of Canaveral. So it was necessary that highly trained individuals take up residence at the Mercury stations around the world to serve as flight controllers. By means of meters and charts of data telemetered down from the spacecraft these individuals monitored the performance of spacecraft and astronaut, and relayed information via teletype back to Canaveral.

Very early in the Mercury series we realized that the fifteen minutes it took to absorb teletype data from distant stations was too long and that it was vital to have voice communications. We set to work to connect the stations and the Canaveral center by high-frequency radio. This type of gear was not very reliable. But HF radio sufficed to provide the necessary control of the Mercury vehicle, with its limited capabilities.

The Mercury's successor, the two-man Gemini, was designed to do a lot more maneuvering. It could change orbit and carry out rendezvous and docking with unmanned Agenas. It was vital therefore that the ground-control center have much more immediate and more reliable data. This meant connecting stations of the worldwide network, first by cable and then by communications satellite.

Finally, in designing the system that would support Apollo missions, it was obvious that the quality of the world network would have to be advanced far beyond even

Gemini's capabilities. That meant using not only high-capacity comsats but also the high-capacity computers needed to process the vast amounts of data that had to be sent. Once such equipment was in operation, it was no longer necessary to dispatch ground controllers to each station.

The progress made since early Mercury days is staggering. For instance, during the seven minutes a Mercury was in range of the station at Carnarvon, Australia, we were able to teletype to Cape Canaveral data summarizing thirty to forty on-board functions. These might include heart beat and respiration of the astronaut, cabin temperature, oxygen supply, etc.

Today, we can get almost instantaneous data at our Houston control center on as many as five hundred gauges, dials or meters. The aeromedical doctor on duty can study the electrocardiogram from each of the three Apollo astronauts as though they were patients in his office. The doctor can speak directly to the astronauts.

The computer used on the ground in the initial control center for Mercury was an adaptation of a computer originally designed with no thought of space flight. It had been designed essentially for scientific projects. It had a storage capacity of 32,000 words, 4,000 fewer than are compressed into each of the miniaturized computers aboard the Apollo modules.

The primary on-the-ground computer used on an Apollo flight has a capacity—an incredible contrast—of 5.5 million words. To the layman, this comparison may seem like a numbers game, and have little impact. But he would understand how phenomenal the advance was if he considered the thousands of man-hours needed to fit together complex equations and endless instructions into a workable set of computer programs for a lunar mission.

A Government-industry team has been working on these programs since 1962. There were times when the task appeared beyond our capability. But the challenge of the presidential appeal to put an American team on the moon in this decade proved sufficient inspiration so that the programming was finally accomplished. It is my opinion that the progress made by the nation in computer technology—spurred primarily, I think, by the space program—is worth a large portion of the dollar outlay for the program. The progress has given us a wealth of knowledge that can be applied to almost every engineering, scientific and industrial endeavor on which we embark.

Though more complex missions have required these great strides in computers, the basic techniques of flight control have remained fundamentally the same from the beginning of our program. Our philosophy requires that we be prepared to handle any emergency. In our mission planning, we go through a painfully thorough process of figuring out the possible contingencies. We call this the "what if" game. And we play it for each different phase of a particular mission.

The mission plan begins with spelling out a basic flight-test objective and working out flight trajectories to carry out the objective. The men in flight operations then analyze each facet of the plan. Of course, it would be impossible to analyze in detail every possible situation. What we do, therefore, is consider the probabilities for particular contingencies, and we plan in greatest detail to handle those emergencies that seem to have the greatest chance of occurring.

The solutions worked out are documented. They are then distributed to the numerous groups who have the most intimate knowledge of the hardware and flight operations for final analysis.

This process culminates in a final trajectory plan and a set of mission rules—a thick volume of "rules of the game" that will govern what we do in particular situations.

For instance, in the final descent of the lunar module to a moon landing, we are critically dependent on a radar system that will determine the precise altitude over the lunar terrain. Normally, the LM [lunar module] must be turned so that the radar is pointing downward by about the time the vehicle has descended to 30,000 feet. It is hoped the radar will promptly start providing accurate altitude readings. However, there is some leeway in the rules. These allow a descent to as low as 13,000 feet without what is called radar lock—in other words, hard evidence that the radar is working perfectly. If it is not, the mission rules say the mission must be aborted. The LM must break off the descent and return to the mother ship.

During the last decade, we have greatly increased our proficiency in contingency studies. But because of the infinite number of possible flight paths, the difficulty of working out mission plans has increased by what engineers call several orders of magnitude. In layman's language, that means it has increased by a factor of hundreds or perhaps thousands.

The approach to developing our lunar-landing capability has not differed widely from the approach used in testing high-speed airplanes. That is, we have attempted to reach our ultimate goal through a step-by-step sequence of missions designed to explore the problems of the various phases of the total lunar mission. Each flight builds on the knowledge gained from the previous one.

## HOUSEHOLD COMPUTERS [5]

Fourteen-year-old Dan Miller likes geometry and pop records, plays golf and tends the family swimming pool. And in his idle moments, he putters around with the family computer.

The Millers, who live in the wooded hills outside Glastonbury, Connecticut, got their computer . . . December 30 [1968].

Since then, Dan has learned to flip its control switches confidently and to operate the teletypewriter that feeds instructions and information into the machine.

He has composed some games and math drills so his sisters, Nancy, thirteen, and Susan, eight, also can match wits

[5] From "Compact Computers," by Scott R. Schmedel, staff reporter. *Wall Street Journal.* p 1+. Ag. 11, '69. Reprinted by permission.

with the computer in keyboard "conversations." One of Dan's computer programs is a variation of an old word game called "hangman," in which a player tries to guess the letters of a word known only to his opponent—and in this case the computer. That program has been accepted for the program library circulated to customers by the computer's maker, Digital Equipment Corporation.

Dan's father, Robert G. Miller, uses the computer too. He's a research statistician employed by a subsidiary of Travelers Corporation, an insurance holding company in nearby Hartford, and he has a variety of personal projects in statistical forecasting that he runs through the computer. But he says he really bought it for his children. "I had wanted to expose my children to the computer," he says. "They'll benefit no matter what they go into."

### An $8,000 Minicomputer

The Millers' computer isn't the big, expensive and formidably complex system that comes most readily to mind at the mention of computers. Their machine is one of a new breed known as minicomputers. It weighs eighty-three pounds and is contained in a black box little bigger than a portable phonograph. Mr. Miller paid just over $8,000 for it.

Not many families are ready to invest in an $8,000 computer, of course. But the advent of the minicomputer has, in just the past few years, made it simple and relatively cheap for rapidly growing numbers of individuals, small businesses, laboratories, schools and other organizations to install their own computers. The minimodels, though capable of doing 333,333 additions a second, are less versatile than standard computers costing anywhere from $42,000 to several million dollars, but most buyers of minicomputers don't need the extra capacity anyway.

Even some giant corporations that already own big computers are finding it economical to scatter minicomputers around rather than tie up their big central computers on small jobs. Engineers and scientists use low-cost desk-side units for help in research and design work, and many small computers are used to monitor and control industrial processes like chemical production and paper-making. Small computers are also often used to screen and prepare data for feeding into big computers.

## Introducing New Users

More significantly, however, the minis are introducing an increasing number of users to computers for the first time.

A minicomputer, for instance, is the heart of an experimental system that New York City schools are using to drill two thousand elementary pupils in arithmetic via telephone connections to their homes. The project, called Dial-A-Drill, serves children from ten schools in Harlem and three other disadvantaged areas, plus about twenty-five children in hospitals and about 180 adults who were intrigued by the possibility of catching up on lost schooling.

One recent Wednesday afternoon, a Dial-A-Drill operator called a boy named Robert at Mount Sinai Hospital and told him it was time for the five-minute session that he has three times a week. Then the recorded voice of the computer took over and asked, "How much is four times two?" Robert's phone and the others used in the project are Touch-Tone models, with buttons instead of dials. He answered the problem by pressing the button marked "8."

The computer automatically stiffens or eases the drill, depending on the accuracy and speed of the answers it gets. It can handle up to sixteen such individualized lessons at one time. "We haven't had any trouble with kids skipping lessons," the project director, Austin W. Sobers, comments. "If we're late calling them, they call us."

## Navigating the QE2

Minicomputers also are being used to help navigate ships. They are the basis, in fact, for new navigation systems using four satellites spinning around the earth.

Navigators of the new luxury liner Queen Elizabeth 2 have such a system. In their chart room behind the liner's bridge is a case about the size of a narrow refrigerator. It contains a minicomputer and a radio receiver that every hour or two picks up signals from one of the satellites. John Fisher, the ship's second officer, says the computer can calculate the liner's position within three hundred to four hundred feet—an extremely accurate means of navigation.

The minis can be used for more prosaic business data processing, too. Liberty Gold Fruit Company, a San Francisco importer and exporter of fruits, canned goods and frozen meats, is converting to a computer from manual equipment for accounting and inventory procedures. "The computer will enable us to add capacity without increasing personnel, and more important, will improve the reliability of our records," says Frank Battat, vice president.

Some business and professional uses of minicomputers have never even been tried with computers before. Donald E. Grampler Realty Inc., a Baltimore-area firm, is developing a computer system intended to match househunters with appropriate homes in the agency's listings.

Dr. Joseph M. Edelman, a Baton Rouge, Louisiana, neurosurgeon, is programming a minicomputer to relieve him and his staff of the time-consuming jobs of dictating and transcribing reports of physical examinations. Dr. Edelman will continue to dictate comments about a patient for typing by a secretary, but he will check off a form when standardized paragraphs can be used to describe normal conditions. A secretary, preparing the final report, can simply type a brief code that will direct the computer to produce the full paragraphs.

Another physician, Dr. Robert M. LaSalle Jr., and a retired electronics engineer, Mark Launder, both of Wabash, Indiana, have created a system that monitors consumption of feed and water by fifty thousand chickens on an egg farm owned by Dr. LaSalle. Keeping track of such details helps farm managers judge whether the birds are feeding properly. The system, which is to be marketed to other poultry farmers by a company called Hupsi Corporation, also will control henhouse heating and cooling equipment.

A minicomputer usually is defined as one with a base price of less than $20,000, although many cost less than $10,000. That covers the central data processor with its internal memory, or data store, and the teletypewriter. Supplemental equipment can lift the price to more than $100,000—which the Dial-A-Drill system costs.

Makers of minicomputers have held prices down partly because of the sharp decline in recent years in the cost of electronic components, particularly the integrated circuits that combine the functions of dozens of individual transistors on a tiny chip. Programming codes have been simplified greatly too. Moreover, minicomputer makers say they don't need to offer the extensive programming, installation and maintenance services required by larger computers.

There's another important factor in cost: Although the minicomputers can be programmed for about any application, they most often are used on a single job. That cuts operating costs to a minimum, because once a unit is programmed the user doesn't have to hire skilled programmers and operators to keep it going. "It's within the capability of any mariner to use this computer, as long as he has five fingers on either hand," says Second Officer Fisher of the Queen Elizabeth 2, referring to the ship's navigation unit.

Clerks are often trained to run minicomputers. "We can take a typist right out of high school and have her producing on our system within an hour," says Victor L. Rosenberg, assistant to the president of Chesapeake Life Insurance Company, which uses a minicomputer to handle the issuance of about one thousand policies a month. Mr. Rosenberg says a typist can become a "competent" operator within a couple of days. "Turnover in personnel doesn't hurt us," he says, "and that was part of our objective."

## THE SUPERTHIEVES [6]

"I could steal a company blind in three months and leave its books looking balanced," boasts Sheldon Dansiger, a burly, thirty-three-year-old data-processing specialist.

His method: Electronic embezzlement. His accomplice: The company's own computer.

Increasingly, business transactions that formerly were recorded on ledger pages are being translated into magnetic impulses in a computer's memory section. It's a simple matter for a crook with technical know-how and a little imagination to program a computer to fleece a company and fool its auditors, according to Mr. Dansiger.

He says corporate executives rarely question the reliability of financial results that emerge from complex, million-dollar machines.

They simply forget that the machines have been built to do whatever the operators direct [explains Mr. Dansiger]. There's nothing to stop them from working quite efficiently for a crook.

### Missing Money

Joseph J. Wasserman, who heads a Bell Telephone Laboratories task force seeking to devise methods of auditing computers used by the Bell System, says many companies already have been hit with heavy losses, but their managements don't know it. He predicts that within a few years someone will uncover a computerized embezzlement that will make even the $150-million salad oil swindle seem puny.

Computers are operating faster and faster and producing fewer and fewer of the printouts that auditors and financial officers need to follow the flow of dollars processed by the machines.

If auditing staffs don't get involved in designing computer systems soon, they might just as well climb up on their stools, pull down their green eyeshades and pray for retirement to come [says Mr. Wasserman].

[6] From "Whir, Blink—Jackpot! Crooked Operators Use Computers to Embezzle Money From Companies," by Alan Adelson, staff reporter. *Wall Street Journal.* 48:1+. Ap. 5, '68. Reprinted by permission.

Others who are aware of the growing problem echo the sentiments of Messrs. Dansiger and Wasserman. "If I were a crook, I'd work through computers," asserts Robert Fano, a leading computer theoretician at Massachusetts Institute of Technology. Ralph Salerno, a former New York City detective who is now a member of a state committee investigating organized crime in New York, says: "I'm not a gambling man, but if I were, I'd bet a month's pay that the Mafia will be working with computers in a few years."

## Bilking a Broker

A number of electronic embezzlements already have come to light. The manager in charge of back-office operations at Walston & Company, a New York brokerage firm, electronically siphoned $250,000 out of the company between 1951 and 1959. By the time the theft was uncovered, the man had become a vice president.

He programmed Walston's computer to transfer money from a company account to two customers' accounts—his and his wife's. The computer was further programmed to show the money had gone to purchase stock for the two accounts. Then he sold the stock supposedly purchased, pocketed the cash and transferred some more.

When a Walston official sensed something was amiss, an examination of the two accounts revealed major irregularities. But the company couldn't figure out the embezzler's system. Because he hadn't stolen any money from customers' accounts,

what he did was absolutely undetectable without internal auditing [says William D. Fleming, Walston president]. Before it happened no one dreamed such a thing was possible, and if he hadn't explained how he did it, we probably still wouldn't know.

The thief explained to Walston's incredulous directors that he pulled off the elaborate money swap by going into the office early Sunday mornings to punch new computer cards and feed them into the machines. "It took someone with absolute knowledge of the computer system to do it," says Mr. Fleming. "This guy was the boss back there. He set up the system and ran the whole show."

## "Anyone Could Do It"

Walston recovered only a fraction of the stolen money. The firm promptly revamped its computer system, instituting a quarterly internal audit and other safeguards designed to foil embezzlement attempts. The former vice president served a year in Sing Sing prison and is now a furniture salesman.

Even as the Walston theft was being uncovered, a similar embezzlement was beginning at another New York brokerage firm, Carlisle & Jacquelin. From 1959 to 1963, the firm's data-processing manager got away with $81,120 by instructing a computer to write checks to fictitious persons and send them to his home address. The scheme was uncovered when the Post Office accidentally returned one of the checks to the firm and the clerk who received it became suspicious.

George Muller, a managing partner of Carlisle & Jacquelin, refused to discuss the case. "We'd have to be crazy to give out all the details now so that anyone who wanted to could do it again," says Mr. Muller. Court records show that the embezzler was convicted, returned the money and received a suspended sentence.

More recently, National City Bank of Minneapolis discovered that the employee who programmed the computerized check-handling system it set up in 1965 embezzled $1,357 over a period of about a year. He programmed the computer to completely disregard his personal checks any time his account had insufficient funds to cover them. The computer allowed each of his bad checks to clear the bank and didn't debit the employee's account for the overdrafts.

The scheme was discovered only by accident, when a computer breakdown forced hand-processing of some checks. One of the embezzler's bad checks bounced. When bank officials confronted him, the employee readily disclosed his scheme. The ex-employee later pleaded guilty, repaid the money and received a suspended sentence.

Computer specialists tell of other ways employees can program computers to steal for them. A crook can change one figure in a computer program, and the machine will report abnormally high inventory losses as normal merchandise breakage, enabling accomplices to steal vast amounts of goods from warehouses without the theft being noticed. Later the operator can remove the evidence simply by putting the original figure back into the computer program.

Computerized payroll systems are potential bonanzas for embezzlers, the experts say. A computer operator can create paychecks for fictitious employees and pay extra overtime and wages to himself quite simply. If he's more ambitious, he can program the computer to deduct a few extra pennies of "income tax" from every paycheck in the plant and pay himself the amount collected.

### Unsafe Safeguards

It's possible to program some safeguards against embezzlement into computers, the specialists say, but the process is complicated and costly and sometimes involves entirely rewriting computer programs and shutting down the machines for a time. Adding safeguards "will cost a company money, and the temptation is often to economize," says Roy Freed, counsel for the computer control division of Honeywell Inc.

But even the most elaborate safeguards might not foil a skilled embezzler. There's always the danger that a crook will come along who's more clever than the specialists who programmed the safeguards into the computer. Lloyd McChesney, chief examiner for the New York Stock Exchange, says that although member firms recently tightened their computer auditing procedures, "no one has yet developed a way to keep his books with a 100 per cent guarantee against embezzlements."

Data-processing specialists, however, say there are a few
basic rules company officials can follow at least to make it
more difficult for a computer crook to raid the corporate
treasury.

A cardinal rule, according to the specialists: Don't let the
computer programmer actually operate the machine. A
crook who can build a loophole into the system and also
feed it the data necessary to carry out his embezzlement
scheme is more likely to succeed than a crook who, after programming the machine, must sit back and hope another
operator will innocently let the machine divert funds to him.

### Computer Sleuthing

Manuel Stonewood—who, with Mr. Dansiger, operates a
New York management consulting and "computer sleuth-
ing" firm called EDP Associates Inc.—says he passed up some
golden opportunities to steal large sums from a major New
York City bank not long ago.

I alone designed a mutual fund's dividend payment system
for the bank, wrote the program for it, then ran the job on the
computer [says Mr. Stonewood].

The operation was so big it had a mistake tolerance of several
hundred thousand dollars. . . . I could have paid at least half that
much to myself in small checks if I had been so inclined, and the
money wouldn't have been missed.

A second rule recommended by the specialists: Segregate
computerized check-writing operations from the departments that authorize checks. This setup makes it difficult for
an embezzler to convert fudged data into actual cash pay-
outs. And it makes it easier for management to spot checks
issued by a computer that has been tampered with.

Another rule: Transfer computer programmers and
operators frequently to different machines and different programs. The theory is that if a crook knows he won't be working on a single job long enough to bilk it for large sums, he's
less likely to go to the trouble of rigging the computer to
steal. Even, if he does rig it, the next man on that job may
spot the embezzlement procedure.

## Phony Facilities

What such safeguards fail to prevent, auditors are supposed to catch, of course. But many data-processing specialists say most auditors don't understand computers, so a clever embezzler can fool them. Some large accounting firms have developed their own highly skilled staffs of computer auditors, but even these specialists can be deceived because so much of what goes on inside the machine never appears on a computer printout.

"Unless you build right into the system a means of printing out audit information, you aren't going to get readable financial records anymore," says Mr. Wasserman of Bell Labs. He says his team of specialists already has developed several new computer auditing techniques that might eventually be used throughout the Bell System.

One technique involves programming a computer to spot seeming irregularities in operating procedures and immediately print out a copy of the questionable transaction for auditors to examine. Another method entails feeding test data into a computer and then checking to determine whether anything interfered with proper processing.

Mr. Wasserman says the Bell System's auditing setup will do far more than spot crooks. For one thing, it will alert executives more quickly to fluctuations in overtime costs, inventory changes and other areas that can have an immediate impact on corporate profits. He says computers currently are used to check the efficiency of telephone operators and to audit employees' calls to guard against widespread misuse of long-distance equipment.

## THE IMPACT OVERSEAS [7]

Fifteen years from now the world's third greatest industrial power, just after the United States and Russia, may

[7] From *The American Challenge*, by J.-J. Servan-Schreiber, French author, publisher, and political philosopher. Copyright © 1967, by Editions Denoel as *Le Défi Américain*. English translation © 1968, 1969 by Atheneum House Inc. Reprinted by permission of Atheneum Publishers.

not be Europe, but *American industry in Europe*. Already, in the ninth year of the Common Market, this European market is basically American in organization.

The importance of U.S. penetration rests, first of all, on the sheer amount of capital invested—currently about $14 billion. Add to this the massive size of the firms carrying out this conquest. Recent efforts by European firms to centralize and merge are inspired largely by the need to compete with the American giants like International Business Machines (IBM) and General Motors. This is the surface penetration. But there is another aspect of the problem which is considerably more subtle.

Every day an American banker working in Paris gets requests from French firms looking for Frenchmen "with experience in an American corporation." The manager of a German steel mill hires only staff personnel "having been trained with an American firm." The British Marketing Council sends fifty British executives to spend a year at the Harvard Business School—and the British government foots the bill. For European firms, so conservative and jealous of their independence, there is now one common denominator: American methods.

During the past ten years Americans in Europe have made more mistakes than their competitors—but they have tried to correct them. And an American firm can change its methods in almost no time, compared to a European firm. The Americans have been reorganizing their European operations. Everywhere they are setting up European-scale headquarters responsible for the firm's continental business, with sweeping powers of decision, and instructions not to pay any attention to national boundaries.

These U.S. subsidiaries have shown a flexibility and adaptability that have enabled them to adjust to local conditions and be prepared for political decisions taken, or even contemplated, by the Common Market.

Since 1958 American corporations have invested $10 billion in Western Europe—*more than a third* of their total investment abroad. Of the six thousand new businesses started overseas by Americans during that period, *half* were in Europe.

One by one, American firms are setting up headquarters to coordinate their activities throughout Western Europe. This is true federalism—the only kind that exists in Europe on an industrial level. And it goes a good deal farther than anything Common Market experts ever imagined.

Union Carbide set up its European headquarters in Lausanne in 1965. The Corn Products Company, which now has ten European branches, moved its coordinating office from Zurich to Brussels and transformed it into a central headquarters. IBM now directs all its European activities from Paris. The Celanese Corporation of America has recently set up headquarters in Brussels; and American Express has established its European central offices in London.

Standard Oil of New Jersey has put its European oil (Esso Europe) headquarters in London, and its European chemical (Esso Chemical SA) command in Brussels. Both have been told to "ignore the present division between the Common Market and the free-trade zone [Britain, Scandinavia]." For Esso, Europe now represents a market *larger than the United States,* and one growing *three times faster.*

Monsanto has moved its international department from St. Louis to Brussels, where Mr. Throdahl, one of its vice presidents, directs not only European operations but all business outside the United States. Monsanto is now building factories in France, Italy, Luxembourg, Britain, and Spain, and preparing plants for Scotland and Ireland. Half of its foreign sales come from Europe.

The greater wealth of American corporations allows them to conduct business in Europe faster and more flexibly than their European competitors. This *flexibility* of the Americans, even more than their wealth, is their major weapon. While Common Market officials are still looking for a law which will permit the creation of European-wide businesses, American firms, with their own headquarters, already form the framework of a real "Europeanization."

A leading Belgian banker recently stated: "The Common Market won't be able to work out a European corporate law in time, and during the next few years U.S. corporations will enjoy a decisive advantage over their European rivals." The American giants in Europe become bigger and stronger all the time, and are hiring "development" experts whose job is to seek new acquisitions.

While all this has been going on, Europeans have done little to take advantage of the new market. On the industrial level Europe has almost nothing to compare with the dynamic American corporations being set up on her soil. The one interesting exception is Imperial Chemical Industries (Britain), the only European firm to establish a continental-scale headquarters to administer its fifty subsidiaries. . . .

During the *past ten years,* from the end of the Cold War and the launching of the first Sputnik, American power has made an unprecedented leap forward. It has undergone a violent and productive internal revolution. Technological innovation has now become the basic objective of economic policy. In America today the government official, the industrial manager, the economics professor, the engineer, and the scientist have joined forces to develop coordinated techniques for integrating factors of production. These techniques have stimulated what amounts to a permanent industrial revolution.

The originality of this revolution consists precisely in the effect this fusion of talents has on decisions made by Government agencies, corporations, and universities. This takes us a long way from the old image of the United States—a country where business was not only separate from government but constantly struggling with it, and where there was a chasm between professors and businessmen. Today, to the contrary, this combination of forces has produced the remarkable integrated entity that John Kenneth Galbraith calls a "technostructure."

If we continue to allow the major decisions about industrial innovation and technological creativity—decisions which directly affect our lives—to be made in Washington, New York, Cambridge, Detroit, Seattle, and Houston, there is a real danger that Europe may forever be confined to second place. We may not be able to build one of those great industrial-intellectual complexes on which a creative society depends. What kind of future do we want?

It is time for us to take stock and face the hard truth. Some of those who watched the decline of Rome or Byzantium also caught a glimpse of the future that was coming. But that was not enough to change the course of history. If we are to be master of our fate, we will need a rude awakening. If this doesn't come, then Europe, like so many other glorious civilizations, will gradually sink into decadence without ever understanding why or how it happened. In 1923 Spengler mused over "The Decline of the West." Today we have barely time enough to comprehend what is happening to us.

What threatens to crush us today is not a torrent of riches, but a more intelligent use of skills. While French, German, or Italian firms are still groping around in the new open spaces provided by the Treaty of Rome, afraid to emerge from the dilapidated shelter of their old habits, American industry has gauged the terrain and is now rolling from Naples to Amsterdam with the ease and the speed of Israeli tanks in the Sinai desert.

Confronted with this conquering force, European politicians and businessmen do not know how to react. Public opinion, confused by their contradictory statements and mysterious shifts of policy, has no way of judging whether American penetration is good or bad.

It is both. The stimulus of competition and the introduction of new techniques are clearly good for Europe. But the cumulative underdevelopment that could transform this assistance into a take-over is bad, very bad.

The danger is not in what the Americans can do, but what the Europeans cannot do, and in the vacuum between the two. This is why the various restrictions and prohibitions that we impose—or would like to impose—are either irrelevant to the problem or deal with it only peripherally. Putting an end to American influence will not fill the vacuum; it will only weaken us further.

While all this is taking place we show no signs of suffering. Our economy grows and our standard of living rises nicely. . . .

The infusion of ever larger amounts of American investment into key industries has the short-term advantage of sparing Europe expensive research costs. But in the long run it deprives the European economy of the possibilities of rapid expansion that exist only in these key industries. The result is to reduce the profitability of exclusively European corporations, which are forced to pay increasingly high royalties for American patents and licenses. In addition to this neocolonial drain on our funds, there are the dividends that are continuously being sent back to the United States. These dividends already exceed the amount of new funds coming into Europe in the form of U.S. capital investments. This is a cumulative snowball phenomenon that is unlikely ever to slow down of its own accord.

The long-term effect of these American investments can be compared to that of the European powers toward their former colonies. When the French built cement plants in Algeria and oil refineries in Senegal they naturally helped diversify the economies of their colonies. But then, even if they wanted to, these colonies could never have achieved industrial development by their own efforts because the mother country controlled the most modern areas of their economies. We can see this operating today.

But Europe is not Algeria or Senegal. If we can build a better industrial organization here in Europe, we will get faster and considerably greater benefits from it than we could from what American investors would leave us after they have drained off dividends and royalties.

It will not be easy to equip ourselves with the tools of management and organization that could make Europe an independent center of industrial and technological creativity. But if we succeed, we will be able to benefit directly from the two principal sources of modern wealth: technological innovation; and the integrated combination of production factors that is the keystone of modern decision-making.

European governments have so far been unwilling to make this effort to catch up, and have not tried to obtain the tools they need for the job.

# V. THE LARGER ISSUES

## EDITOR'S INTRODUCTION

The extraordinary quality of the computer impact is that it is an ongoing phenomenon. Computers breed more knowledge and information. The output can be plugged back into the computer's memory, thus making for a smarter computer. This has a profound effect on our mode of life because as knowledge advances we change not only our way of doing things but also the way we think about them.

This section deals with some of the key areas of concern that the ongoing computer revolution is affecting, some of the questions it raises, and what solutions may be in store.

The first article in the section, by Vance Packard, notes that the computer's ability to keep and process endless amounts of information threatens our right to privacy. Already it is being proposed that every relevant fact about our lives should be stored in some huge, central computer. Is there a danger here? Is this desirable?

The next article explains the possibility—and desirability —of a national electronic information service. It stresses the danger of believing, needlessly, that robotism is inevitable.

The third article comes to grips with other broad moral issues. It notes that people are already searching for new meanings and values that will be valid in the changed environment.

The article that follows addresses itself to still another concomitant of this ongoing revolution. Can machines think? it asks. Fortunately for all of us, the conclusion is that computers can't do any more than they are told to do.

But while machines may never think, it is clear they are accelerating change far beyond what most human beings have been accustomed to. The next selection thus asks, "Can

Man Keep Up?" No doubt he can, but not without a good deal of effort. And so the final article in the section notes that it is a reasonable assumption that in the future most people will have to go back to school many times in the course of their lives.

## DON'T TELL IT TO THE COMPUTER[1]

Consider the trail of records most of us leave behind in this increasingly statistical age. Our birth is recorded not only on a birth certificate but also on our parents' income-tax return. Nongovernment file keepers have information on our income, home value, debts and banks, data we often surrender when we apply for credit. There are the reports investigators make to insurance companies, which may include appraisals of our social and sex lives as well as our financial stability. Employment files have results of personality inventories and lie-detector tests. Hospital records list our medical history, and moving companies have prudently made inventories of our possessions.

State and local governments have our school records, including our grades, IQ scores and any reports of emotional difficulties. At least one government agency will have records of our driving brushes with the law, property holdings and licenses (including marriage and divorce papers).

The Federal Government has our tax returns, our responses to the increasingly lengthy Census questionnaires, our Social Security record, our application for a passport, and perhaps our fingerprints. If we have been in military service, worked for a defense contractor or for the Government, there are lengthy files on us that may well indicate known associates, affiliations and religious beliefs. If we have applied for an FHA loan on a home there will usually be an estimate of

[1] From article by Vance Packard, author of *The Naked Society*, a study of the invasions of privacy by government and other interests. New York *Times Magazine*. p 44+. Ja. 8, '67. © 1967 by The New York Times Company. Reprinted by permission.

our marriage prospects. And this is just a small part of the total.

The citizen concerned about the erosion of his privacy has until now had some consolation in knowing that all these records about his life have been widely dispersed and often difficult to get at. Digging up a sizable file on any individual has been time-consuming and expensive. But today, with the advent of giant sophisticated computers capable of storing and recalling vast amounts of information, this consolation is vanishing.

And now the Federal Government is seriously considering the establishment of a national electronic data center, which would combine in a single computer system information on American citizens that is now scattered around twenty different Federal agencies. The center would allow various officials and outside researchers push-button access to a great mass of consolidated information.

The idea for a central data bank began in a committee of the Social Science Research Council, which recommended in April 1965, "that the Bureau of the Budget, in view of its responsibility for the Federal statistical program, immediately take steps to establish a Federal Data Center." The White House, reacting favorably, thereupon set up a special task force headed by Dr. Carl Kaysen, of Princeton's Institute for Advanced Study, to examine the concept.

The Kaysen report, submitted to the White House in November, unequivocally urged such a center. In fact it called for a startling expansion of the proposed National Data Center to include information from state and local data-gathering agencies as well. It argued that the present Federal system of getting and using statistics was obsolete, both "inadequate—in the sense of failing to do things that should and could be done—and inefficient—in the sense of not doing what it does at minimum cost." A national data bank would give both governmental and academic analysts a much sharper view of the nation's problems and possibilities—for instance, by relating employment data now isolated in the Labor Department with industrial output information now kept by the Federal Reserve.

In discussing the hot issue of how far such a data center would reach into an individual's life, Washington officials are somewhat vague. For example, Raymond T. Bowman, Assistant Director for Statistical Standards of the Budget Bureau and the man responsible for making recommendations on the data center, has claimed that

a statistical data center would not have an interest in building up dossiers on individuals because statistical interests do not center on individual cases. . . . I would not want to say that within the data center . . . there would be no identification of information with an individual. . . . You would not be able to use this information meaningfully unless this kind of identification were maintained.

And an adviser of his has been quoted in the Washington *Post* as arguing that valuable information is lost if confidences are kept and statistics are made anonymous too early in the game.

The dangers in allowing the Federal Government to assemble information on individual citizens in a single center are almost self-evident.

We know today that information is power. As Dr. Robert Morison, scientific director for the Rockefeller Foundation, has put it: "We are coming to recognize that organized knowledge puts an immense amount of power in the hands of the people who take the trouble to master it." Bernard S. Benson, a computer expert, has conceded that the concentration of power in the form of accumulated information can be "catastrophically dangerous."

Experts in computer technology who testified in July before the Special Subcommittee on Invasion of Privacy of the House Committee on Government Operations indicated that a central data center could easily be converted into a more ominous dossier bank. The same technology that enables the machine to process information about individuals could be used for the instant retrieval of information on any one of them.

Indeed, we should be uneasy right now about the vast amount of information that the Federal Government is starting to store away on its citizens in dossiers, card files and electronic memory banks.

The Government has led the way in installing bigger and more sophisticated computers, purchasing many thousands of them, including some of the world's largest. The Civil Service Commission is now operating a center to train 2,300 Federal employees to get maximum usable information out of various computer systems.

The Internal Revenue Service, too, has made a massive investment in computers to store and assess information on taxpayers. We can all be cheered by the promised increase in fairness and efficiency that theoretically will result, but the prospect is disquieting. For the electronic memory banks can presumably store a cumulative file (or "cum") covering up to ten years of each taxpayer's life. The vast amount of information he has provided about himself, his family and his business dealings over a decade would be subject to virtually instant retrieval. In short, IRS computers will be able instantly to dredge up dimly remembered personal affairs of the past.

Federal agencies have also developed increasingly systematic patterns for exchanging information. When a Federal agent makes a National Agency Check on a person, for example, he customarily checks the files of at least eight Federal agencies. A congressional investigator reported that results of lie-detector tests taken by one agency were freely passed around to personnel officials in other agencies. And we know that various Government units are developing a central information center to exchange information on individuals involved in criminal investigations.

Unless safeguards are developed, the Government will be increasingly inclined to assemble more and more specific data about specific individuals. When the Social Security program began we were assured that our Social Security number would be kept secret, that no one could possibly use it to keep track of our movements. Today, we must not only write our Social Security number on our income tax return but supply it to banks and employers. Social Security numbers are in fact so easily obtainable that one nationwide investigating firm has a line on its standard form for the Social Security number of the person under investigation.

On top of that, the Census Bureau has now suggested that the 1970 census include every responder's Social Security number—for the express purpose of aiding the correlation of Federal information. So the Social Security number could become not only public information but the key to creating a frightening dossier on each individual.

Or consider the Census. The Constitution calls for an "enumeration" of the population every ten years, but today the Census has gone far beyond that. Many millions of citizens in 1960 had to answer 165 questions about their lives, purchasing habits and incomes. The pressure is on to add a host of new inquiries, such as ethnic origins, religious affiliations, schooling and the like to the 1970 Census.

And failure to answer every question on the Census can result in a fine or jail sentence. This was made clear after the 1960 Census when William F. Rickenbacker of Briarcliff Manor, New York, was fined $100 and given a suspended jail sentence for refusing on grounds of principle to fill out the household Census form.

In all the discussion of plans for a national data center, it seems to me that the crucial question is whether we are letting technology get out of hand without a sufficient concern for human values. To my mind there are four major dangers in allowing governmental machines to pool and exchange data on individual Americans; the first two concern the nation as a whole, the others the individual citizen.

First, a central data bank threatens to encourage a depersonalization of the American way of life. Americans increasingly, and rightly, resent their being numbers controlled by a computer. Students at the vast state universities resent having their exams machine graded and their ID numbers often printed twice as large as their names. Much of the same resentment may be felt by some of the hundreds of thousands of applicants for Federal jobs who find not only that their exams are machine graded but also that an automated machine writes the letter telling them whether or not they have passed the test.

Second, the central data bank is likely to increase the distrust of citizens in their own Government and alienate them from it. People will be wary of what they tell the Government if they discover that information confided for one purpose is used to affect their life in some entirely different connection. If what they tell the FHA to get a home loan prevents them from getting a job with a Government contractor they will start being distrustful.

The Kaysen report did recognize that if Federal information on individuals is thus centralized the citizens ought to be given assurance that it cannot somehow be used against them, or otherwise falsification might become rampant. But such an assurance—especially in view of the existing "credibility gap"—might have little effect, for any evidence that the Administration was increasing its power over the citizenry by centralizing files on more than 100 million citizens would inevitably create disquiet.

In addition, the public will inevitably feel a suffocating sense of surveillance. One of the hallmarks of totalitarianism has been this sense that somewhere there is an all-seeing eye.

Third, a central file can absorb large batches of data about people but it is ill-equipped to correct errors, allow for extenuating circumstances, or bring facts up to date.

An acquaintance discovered quite by accident that his local credit bureau, in a litigation report on him, said he had been the target of three lawsuits for failure to meet commitments; on the record he obviously was a bad credit risk. In fact, the first case was a $5 scare suit back in the1930s over a magazine subscription he had never ordered; the second involved a disagreement over a $200 lawyer's fee and was later compromised amicably; the third concerned a disputed fee he had charged a client, and this suit he won in court. It took my friend two days of digging to clear his record with the credit bureau.

Many employers, including the Federal Government, require a job applicant to note if he has ever been held by a law-enforcement agency for investigation. Obviously hundreds of thousands of citizens have been momentarily held and then released without charges—but it is hard to explain innocent circumstances to a computer.

Even more serious is the computer's inability to recognize that people indeed often do change and become more responsible as they grow up. The son of a friend of mine in a midwestern city applied to several department stores in the area for a job when he was graduated from high school at the age of eighteen. He had recommendations from his minister, scoutmaster, high school principal and chief of police. But no store would even give his application serious consideration, since it turned out that his name was in the stores' central file of known lawbreakers. Five years earlier, at the age of thirteen, the boy had been caught snitching two dollars' worth of fishline.

America's frontiers were settled by people seeking to make a fresh start, escaping the unpleasantness of the past. Today, with central files and computers increasingly recording the past, the possibility of a fresh start is becoming increasingly difficult. The notion of the possibility of redemption is likely to be incomprehensible to the computer.

The most disquieting hazard in a central data bank would be the placing of so much power in the hands of the people in a position to push computer buttons. When the details of our lives are fed into a central computer or other vast file-keeping systems, we all fall under the control of the machine's managers to some extent.

In recent years we have seen at least one notable case in Washington of information from a secret dossier being used

in an effort to intimidate and discredit a person making statements embarrassing to certain high officials. He was an insurance man in the Washington area who had disclosed some
curious insurance practices in connection with the Bobby
Baker case.

The filekeepers of Washington have derogatory information on literally millions of citizens. The more it is fed into
central files, the greater the danger that it will be used as a
form of control.

One computer scientist, Eldridge Adams, has warned that
the electronic computer systems being used by Government
agencies were collecting so much information about families
and individuals that those controlling the machines were
achieving "truly frightening" power. He indicated that without proper control the computers would convert our society
into the Big Brother regime predicted in Orwell's *1984*.

Let us remember, 1984 is only . . . [a few] years away. My
own hunch is that Big Brother, if he comes to the United
States, will turn out to be not a greedy power-seeker but a
relentless bureaucrat obsessed with efficiency. And he, more
than the simple power-seeker, could lead us to that ultimate
of horrors, a humanity in chains of plastic tape. . . .

There is some question whether the Administration could
informally establish a National Data Center without specific
enabling legislation by Congress. In the past, Congress has
become aware of projects involving privacy invasion—such
as the Executive Department's purchase of lie-detector and
surveillance equipment—only after they had been well established.

In July [1966] . . . [Representative Cornelius E. Gallagher
(Democrat, New Jersey), chairman of the House invasion-of-
privacy subcommittee] told of reports that the Budget Bureau had already tentatively earmarked funds that might be
used to start a data-bank program. Later, an official of the
Budget Bureau advised me that if plans go forward to create
such a program there will first be a request put to Congress

for an appropriation. But apparently the groundwork for a central data center of some sort has already been well laid. The Kaysen report mentioned that "a sufficient beginning has been made . . . to permit the center a running start."

At subcommittee hearings, the Budget Bureau's Raymond Bowman suggested that safeguards could be established to prevent the "release" of information on individual citizens or businesses. But prohibitions against release become somewhat irrelevant—and their real effectiveness somewhat dubious—if officials at all twenty contributing agencies are permitted to have push-button access to the central bank.

While it may seem obvious to a layman that each contributing agency could be required to remove all identification of individuals or businesses before sending its statistics on to the central bank, Budget Bureau experts raise practical objections. Bowman said flatly, "It is not possible to have a meaningful data center in which the identity of the individual is deleted." For one thing, apparently, the elimination of identification would complicate the problem of "meshing" the data correctly in the first place and perhaps make impossible the adding and assigning of new data on individuals as they come in over the years. Also, there is the practical objection that the mechanics of removing identifications would multiply the costs of setting up the system.

The task force report spoke of the importance of developing (unspecified) safeguards against unwarranted disclosure or publication of information about individuals or enterprises. It mentioned vaguely that at some stage in setting up the center thought would need to be given to protecting the confidentiality of the data and acknowledged that "the question of the proper or improper use of information by different agencies is indeed a ticklish one."

But at no point did it attempt to propose specifically how foolproof safeguards could be established, and even confessed its incompetence to be precise on such matters. It mentioned only that there might be "standards of disclosure," "techniques for preserving confidentiality," "recodification" of laws and rules, procedures for "screening," and so on.

It is not enough to talk in generalities of eventual safeguards. Could the public ever conceivably be fully protected from abuses and mistakes? What assurance would the public have that administrative techniques, standards, rules, etc. would not be quietly changed in some future regime reaching for greater power over the citizenry? Only a carefully drawn Federal law—enacted before the data center is established— would seem to offer any protection at all for the long term.

As Chairman Gallagher has said: "Merely stating that rules, laws, individual judgment and congressional-executive action should be exerted to safeguard privacy does not provide the solution."

There appears, then, to be an impasse here between the desires of the statisticians and the fears of the civil libertarians. Quite possibly it can be resolved only by abandoning the whole project or by persuading the statisticians to settle for a more modest exchange of depersonalized statistics.

(Or, interestingly enough, by technology itself. Congressman Gallagher says: "Latest refinements of modern hardware make the centralization of data dubious, rather than obvious." Experts suggest, he says, that "it might be more advantageous to build a decentralized computer system to solve the growing information-gathering crisis. Under such a system, the data could remain with the various agencies and would be fed into a central computer for statistical analysis.")

At times Administration statisticians have seemed bewildered that anyone would doubt their good intentions and their willingness to impose regulations on their procedures. A sharp answer to this comes from Charles A. Reich, professor of constitutional law at Yale University: "I believe that the real protection in this world comes not from people's good intentions but from laws."

Looking at the broader problems Reich has argued that it is time to pass laws stipulating the kinds of questions that cannot be asked of any citizen. "A person has the right not to be defamed," he maintains "whether it is by a machine or a man."

I believe it is time, too, that Congress, in consultation with Federal regulatory agencies, moves to establish closer control over the vast empires of private and cooperative businesses engaged in investigating citizens: the credit bureaus, insurance investigating firms and private-investigating enterprises. Several of these businesses gross from $40 million to $125 million a year from the sale of personal information. Since the information gathered by these enterprises crosses state lines there seems to be clear congressional jurisdiction.

In any event, Congress should soon start weighing the advantages to society of consolidating statistics against the very real threat that central data systems can imperil personal privacy, and in fact can become instruments of control over American citizens.

## POWER TOOLS FOR THINKING [2]

It is becoming common to envisage man in the future as an anonymous cog in a vast interconnection of machines, cables, signals and moving vehicles—all controlled by computers.

In this picture of the coming world, every action of society, down to its infinite detail, will be planned and preset. Man will be a mere number turned up by the computer. He will be a docile, instructed participant in the operations of the economy and an apathetic, nonparticipating, disinterested bystander in the decisions. It will be difficult to distinguish man from machine.

Yet the same system that can tell millions of people exactly what to do, as though they were robots, can just as well ask them to choose what they prefer to do from a group of well-presented alternatives. In this case, the citizens of the

[2] From "Computers: Power Tools for Thinking," by Dr. Simon Ramo, vice chairman of the board, TRW, Inc. *Christian Science Monitor*. p 9. Jl. 27, '67. Reprinted by permission from *The Christian Science Monitor*. © 1967 The Christian Science Publishing Society. All rights reserved.

future would be able to tune in on the discussion of issues, they would take part by expressing their reactions electronically in two-way communication from their homes. The results, automatically and speedily processed by computer, would be disclosed to all and used in the deliberations of the Congress, the state legislatures, and the city councils.

I am not suggesting that it would be to our advantage to have every citizen share in every decision that affects each complex operation of our nation. However, the decision as to whether we move toward a robot society or, instead, in the direction of "on-line democracy" or toward any form or variation in between is not made by technology. It is made, in the end, by the people who create and use that technology.

Technology can make possible a more informed, more interested, more active citizenry, if people want it to. It can facilitate the tapping and using of citizen opinion on issues as a way of life. It can create new, powerful citizen participation in decision making at a level not imagined in the previous "pretechnological-society" history of man.

Forebodings of a robotlike society arise because of what technologists tell us is possible. They soon will be able to forge a pervasive, automatic, electronic information system that will sense all the data needed to control our daily operations. Next it will process this information on a mass scale in accordance with all-embracing programs. Finally it will communicate this information everywhere to the cooperative, responding machines and men.

Production, distribution, accounting, transportation, banking, education, government, lawmaking, engineering, medicine, and most other operations and pursuits of man will be altered in their organization and practice. As the role of the human participant in the gathering, flow, contemplation, and use of the information that keeps the world going becomes a job for the electronic machine, the need for a new man-machine partnership emerges.

This is why the advent of the computer age appears to some to carry the threat of the long-dreaded planned economy.

I submit there is a much more likely and attractive path. It leads to a free market of a new form and unprecedented level.

## Robotism Works Both Ways

To explore this route, let us note first a rather general technological-social point.

A ubiquitous electronic information network can make possible a robot society. This is because all the information needed for control—from airplane schedules to pickle distribution—is at the right place at the right time. Yet from this it follows, in principle, that the technology can also be used to enhance democracy and free enterprise. The choice depends on our understanding of the dynamics of technology and matching social advance to technological advance so we can beneficially exploit it.

More specifically, an advanced computer-and-communication technology would make it possible to give every citizen all the information he should consider for the democratic selection of goals. Such a national information network could both inform and gather opinions and process these for the making of decisions.

To assume a future robot society is to assume also the design, production, and installation of millions of economical, reliable, interconnected electronic devices placed everywhere. But if truly available, they can equally well be used to make possible individual participation, in our homes, in a form of "instant democracy"—if this is what we desire.

## Controls Have Their Limits

As to the feared planned economy, it cannot really be successful in controlling things in detail unless the consumer is in the communications loop. Perhaps the Soviet Union has proved this point by demonstrating that, although the government can plan what to produce, it cannot force the citizens to use the products.

Again, if a computer network can communicate with everyone to ensure the working of the economy, it can also ask everyone what he wants.

The essence of true, free enterprise is the free market. As a matter of fact, it exists only in part today in the United States. The more that people are really free to choose how they will spend their money, the more that the producer is willing and able to offer his ideas and goods for sale in the free market, then the closer we come to realizing the full potential of free enterprise.

If the gathering and flow of, and access to, all information pertaining to the market and its products can be automated, then free enterprise should become freer. The computer network should be able to step up the process of consumer selection. It should speed decisions on capital risk or investment. It should implement responsive production and distribution.

This could be a free market of a form and at a peak civilization has never before known. It could be a market in which everyone would know quickly what is available and, beforehand, what might later be available. It would be a market in which a proposal to produce something of possible interest could be quickly considered by potential buyers.

Each of us in our own homes could respond electronically and directly to a commercial that offered contemplated automobile models with a substantial discount for orders placed well ahead.

We could step to our consoles and push the right buttons to make our purchases. Our bank accounts would be reduced electronically, and an addition would be made to the assets of the company making the offer.

This kind of direct consumer information and marketing could be used by the network's clients to schedule manufacturing and distribution in detail. This would greatly improve efficiency in every industrial activity from the ordering of basic raw materials to the setting up and manning of plants, facilities, and transportation. . . .

The entrepreneur and the consumer together would be involved in an "on-line" market exchange.

### Risk Could Be Shared

This would be superior to the nineteenth century form of free enterprise, which involves taking the complete risk, with little consumer involvement, before the market offer can be made.

Capital investment and risk in an environment of fast-responding, electronically informed, interested, and active customers would be something new. The profit-to-risk ratio would rise. With the opportunity for individual participation in such an accelerating free-enterprise system, enthusiastic response to this path might be expected to follow, both for the customers and for the investors. More efficient scheduling for production and distribution would leave more resources for risk taking.

Rapid dissemination of ideas for new products and quick follow-up into production of the popular proposals would act to stimulate other ideas. So creativity, imagination, and optimum application of resources—in the sense of direct response to public will—would all be enhanced.

A role for government would exist in such a computerized free-enterprise economy. But it would not be as a rival to the private-economy sector. The government would have a more natural part to play. In fact, it would have its hands full under strong public pressure to provide an ever-broadening service to the consumer, to enable more and more products and services to be offered on the computerized free market.

### Rules Would Be Needed

The government would not have to create the system. But it would have to set the rules. It would have to referee, license, and ensure objectivity and fair opportunity in the workings of the free market's computerized national electronic information service.

Further expansions, to enable the broadest participation in the free market by both consumers and risk-taking suppliers, would probably be demanded faster than the government could do its part. The government thus would probably become the bottleneck. This should lessen the worry about possible government effort to plan the economy from the top.

Aided itself by computer-based information on the total progress of the economy, the government may be in a position in the future to do well the one function related to economic planning that it is now trying to do—and so far doing rather poorly: This is the adjustment of fiscal and monetary policy so as to assist in the attainment of maximum growth and minimum instabilities in the progress of the economy. . . .

Science and technology, in this instance as in every other, offer us choices. They do not determine the direction in which our society must go. The danger is that we may come to believe the myth that robotism is inevitable. We may lose the chance to shape our future by default if we fail to provide the social arrangements and innovations to employ technological advance so as to attain the civilization we want.

## THE SEARCH FOR MEANING AMID CHANGE [3]

What makes America unique in our time is that it is the first society to experience the future. It is becoming a *technetronic* society—a society that is shaped culturally, psychologically, socially and economically by the impact of technology and electronics, particularly computers and communications.

[3] From article by Zbigniew Brzezinski, professor of government and director of the Research Institute on Communist Affairs at Columbia University. New York *Times.* p C 141+. Ja. 6, '69. © 1969 by The New York Times Company. Reprinted by permission.

This movement beyond the industrial phase is separating America from the rest of the world, prompting a further fragmentation among an already differentiated mankind.

The transition to the new age is not easy. Changes produce tensions, while the very novelty of our contemporary experience is inimical to established solutions and tested programs. As a result, American society is troubled and some parts of it are even tormented. The social blinders are being ripped off and a sense of inadequacy is becoming more widespread.

The spread of literacy, and particularly the access to colleges and universities of about 40 per cent of our youth, has created a large intellectual constituency which rejects the complacent belief in the spontaneous goodness of American social change. At the same time, the difficulty of knowing what ought to be done is magnified by the novelty of America's problem. Turning to nineteenth century ideologies is not the answer—and it is symptomatic that the New Left has found it most difficult to apply the available, particularly Marxist, doctrines to our new reality.

The search for meaning is characteristic of the present American scene. It could portend most divisive and bitter ideological conflicts, especially as intellectual disaffection becomes linked with the increasing bitterness of the deprived Negro masses. If carried to its extreme, this could bring to America a phase of violent, intolerant and destructive civil strife, combining ideological and racial intolerance.

However, it would be highly misleading to construct a one-sided picture of the future, with the stress on violence, crisis and failure. The changes transforming American society are contradictory, and their outcome depends largely on how we ourselves harness the powers and the means that the technetronic age puts at our disposal.

Thus, in the political sphere, the increased flow of information and more efficient techniques of instant coordination need not necessarily prompt greater concentration of power within some ominous control agency distantly located

at the governmental apex. On the contrary, these developments also make possible greater devolution of authority and
responsibility to the lower levels of government and society,
making self-government for the first time really technically
possible.

Today, the university is the creative eye of the massive
communications complex, the source of much strategic planning, domestic and international. Its engagement in the
world is encouraging the appearance of a new breed of poli-
ticians-intellectuals, men who make it a point to mobilize
and draw on the most expert, scientific and academic advice
in the development of their political programs. The ideo-
logically minded intellectual dissenter, who saw his role
largely in terms of proffering dogmatic social critiques, is
rapidly being displaced either by experts and specialists, who
become involved in special governmental undertakings, or
by generalists-integrators.

## Use of Social Talent

In these conditions, power will gravitate increasingly into
the hands of those who control the information and can correlate it most rapidly. Our existing postcrisis management
institutions will probably be increasingly supplanted by pre-
crisis management institutions, the task of which will be to
identify in advance likely social crises and to develop programs to cope with them. In that setting, the key to successful
adaptation to the new conditions will be found in the effective selection, distribution and utilization of social talent.
By 1980, not only will approximately two thirds of United
States urban dwellers be college-trained, but it is most certain
that systematic élite retraining will be standard in the political system.

The increasing gross national product, which by the end
of the century could reach approximately $10,000 income per
capita a year, linked with educational advance, could prompt
among those less involved in social management and less interested in scientific development a wave of interest in the

cultural and humanistic aspects of life, in addition to purely hedonistic preoccupations. The achievement-oriented society might give way to the amusement-focused society, with essentially spectator events (mass sports and TV) providing an opiate for increasingly purposeless masses.

But while for the masses life will grow longer and time will seem to expand, for the activist élite time will become a rare commodity. . . .

Already now, speed dictates the pace of our lives, instead of the other way around. As the speed of transportation increases—largely by its own technological momentum—man discovers that he has no choice but to avail himself of that acceleration, either to keep up with others or because he thinks he can thus accomplish more. This will be especially true of the élite, for whom an expansion in leisure time does not seem to be in the cards. Thus as speed expands, time contracts, and the pressures on the élite increase.

Accordingly, it will be essential to put much higher emphasis on human values lest personal existence become increasingly depersonalized. There is the real danger that human conduct will become less spontaneous and less mysterious: more predetermined and subject to deliberate programming.

### Man's Powers Expand

Man will increasingly possess the capacity to determine the sex of his children, to affect through drugs the extent of their intelligence and to modify and control their personalities. The human brain will acquire expanded powers, with computers becoming as routine an extension of man's reasoning as automobiles have been of man's mobility. The human body will be improved and its durability extended. . . . The prolongation of life will alter our mores, our career patterns and our social relationships.

New forms of social control may be needed to limit the indiscriminate exercise by individuals of their new powers. The possibility of extensive chemical mind control, the danger of loss of individuality inherent in extensive transplantation, and the feasibility of manipulation of the genetic structure will call for a social definition of common criteria of restraint as well as of utilization.

## Manmade Environment

By the end of this century the citizens of the more developed countries will live predominantly in cities, hence almost surrounded by manmade environment. Confronting nature could be to them what facing the elements was to our forefathers—meeting the unknown and not necessarily liking it. Our descendants will be shaped almost entirely by what they themselves create and control. Precisely because of this we will have to define more deliberately the quality of life that we seek.

In the industrial society, technical knowledge was applied primarily to one specific end: the acceleration and improvement of production techniques. Social consequences were a later by-product of this paramount concern. In the technetronic society, scientific and technological knowledge, in addition to enhancing productive capabilities, quickly spills over to affect directly almost all aspects of life.

Accordingly, the emerging technetronic society will differ from the industrial one in a variety of economic, political and social aspects. The following examples may be briefly cited to summarize some of the contrasts:

In an industrial society, the mode of production shifts from agriculture to industry, with the use of muscle and animals supplanted by machine-operation. In the technetronic society, industrial employment yields to services, with automation and cybernetics replacing individual operation of machines.

Problems of employment and unemployment yield to questions relating to skill-obsolescence, security, vacations, leisure, and psychic well-being of relatively secure but potentially aimless lower-middle-class blue-collar workers.

Education, no longer merely concerned with overcoming illiteracy or with technical training, becomes universal, highly advanced and relies more on visual and audial devices. It becomes extended in time and it is to be expected that in our lifetime refresher courses throughout the span of one's life will replace the present reliance on a self-contained decade and a half of formal education.

Traditional urban political élites are increasingly replaced by professional political leadership possessing special technical skills, relying on intellectual talents and exploiting mass media to mobilize individual support directly, no longer by the intermediary of organized parties.

In the technetronic society the university becomes an intensely involved think-tank, the source of much sustained political planning and social innovation and no longer a withdrawn ivory tower.

## Great Question Posed

The search for broad ideological answers, typical of the early stage of industrialization, gives way to a more pragmatic problem-solving approach to social issues, though that approach is not devoid of idealistic concern with human values.

Whatever the outcome, American society is the one in which the great questions of our time will be first tested through practice: Can the individual and science coexist, or will the dynamic momentum of the latter fundamentally alter the former? Can man, living in the scientific age, grow in intellectual depth and philosophical meaning, and thus in his personal liberty too? Can the institutions of political democracy be adapted to the new conditions sufficiently quickly to meet the crises, yet without debasing their democratic character?

Because the problems that America faces are unique to America only in their timing, it may be appropriate to stimulate, for the first time on a global scale, the much-needed dialogue on what it is about man's life that we wish to safeguard or to promote, and on the relevance of existing moral systems to an age that cannot be fitted into the narrow confines of fading doctrine.

## Differences Widen

More generally, we will have to find a way of avoiding somehow the widening of the cultural and psychosocial gap inherent in the growing differentiation of the world. Even with gradual differentiation throughout human history, it was not until the industrial revolution that sharp differences between societies began to appear. Today, some nations still live not unlike the pre-Christian times, many no better than in the medieval age. Yet soon a few will live in ways so new that it is now difficult to imagine their social and individual ramifications.

If the developed world takes a leap—as seems inescapably the case—into a reality that is even more different from ours today than ours is from that of an Indian village, the gap, and its concomitant strains, will not narrow.

On the contrary, the instantaneous electronic intermeshing of mankind will make for an intense confrontation straining social and international peace. In the past, differences were livable because of the time and distance that separated them. Today, these differences are actually widening, while techtronics are eliminating the two insulants of time and distance.

The resulting trauma could create almost entirely different perspectives on life, with insecurity, envy and hostility becoming the dominant emotions for increasingly large numbers of people. A three-way split into rural-backward, urban-industrial and technetronic ways of life can only further divide men, intensify the existing difficulties to global understanding and give added vitality to latent or existing conflicts.

## CAN MACHINES THINK? [4]

Can a computing machine be taught to think in the broadest sense, as the human brain can think and learn? Efforts have been made in this direction, based on accumulating knowledge of how the human brain works. The brain is, in effect, a whole hierarchy of computers with much of its basic input provided by ranks of lesser computers down the line. The information gathered by the retina of the eye, for instance, is not simply shunted along to the brain. Instead, the retina acts like a tiny, highly sophisticated computer, analyzing the visual data and passing on only the significant results. In the brain itself further analysis takes place as information moves from one level to another and is processed in computerlike fashion all along the way until a unified perception results.

In a computer, electric pulses travel to specific places along specific conduits to produce their own version of a unified perception in the form of an answer. Not so in the brain. One brain cell, or neuron, may pulse another, as the electronic switches in a computer pulse each other, but the similarity ends there. Each neuron has inputs from a number of other nerve cells, so that in one way or another all the 10 billion or so neurons in the brain are interconnected directly or indirectly. The system provides whole arrays of incredibly complex feedback loops in which some cells qualify the operations of others, stimulating them to respond to certain incoming signals and inhibiting their responses to others.

Theoretically it would be possible, as one computer scientist has noted, to hook together hierarchies of computers to simulate the complex layers of the brain. The gear necessary to give this supercomputer even one twentieth of a human brain's capacity would fill several barns. And the fact is that no one would really know how to hook together such an array. Scientists have a general idea about how the brain

[4] "The Eerie Interface of Man and Machine," by Robert Campbell. *Life.* 63:72. O. 27, '67. © 1967 Time Inc.

functions, but a wiring diagram, or anything like it, is almost
totally lacking and seems likely to remain elusive for a long
time to come. Even if a wiring diagram came to hand, the
problem of writing a program for such a contraption would
present an equally enormous obstacle. Reflecting on the difficulties, a veteran programmer said:

> It takes us fifteen to twenty years to program our children.
> And they can *really* learn—sometimes. But with the kind of ma-
> chine you're talking about, you would have to feed in millions of
> separate little things every day to equal what a child takes in. And
> after three years of this kind of business, it still might not have
> learned to reason or work out its own programs. You ask it to add
> 2 and 2, and maybe it says 5.

Since "thinking" is apparently not a prospect—at least
not until the brain is better understood or a major new
breakthrough revolutionizes computer technology again—
computers will remain painfully literal-minded. One important word in the lexicon of computer programmers is GIGO,
which simply means: Garbage In, Garbage Out—that is, if
the wrong information is put into the machine, the results
will also be wrong. The computer has no sense that it is
being fed garbage, and anyone who gets about much on the
computer circuit is bound to hear some rich examples of
GIGOism.

At Cape Kennedy some time ago a rocket rose majestically
from its launch pad and headed toward Venus. But following
lift-off it began to wobble uncontrollably and had to be destroyed after only 293 seconds of flight. What had happened
to $18.5 million worth of hardware was that a programmer
omitted a minor item from the long list of explicit instructions to the computer that was "flying" the bird.

The missed item was a hyphen, and its omission led the
computer into the same sort of misunderstanding that leav-
ing the hyphen out of a phrase involving "fifty-five gallon
drums" might have on a human.

When astronauts L. Gordon Cooper and Charles Conrad
splashed down 103 miles off target on August 29, 1965, it was

no fault of theirs or of their computer. The flight, including reentry, was computer guided. In determining the exact time for firing retro rockets, the programmer had assumed that the earth revolved exactly once every 24 hours, whereas in fact—as we know from having to squeeze in a whole extra day every fourth year—it makes a shade more than one revolution in that time. But if you're orbiting the earth many times and someone fires the retros exactly at 1:51 P.M., after figuring on a day of precisely twenty-four hours, you can wind up out of touch with the earth by a significant number of earthy miles—which is just what happened to astronauts Cooper and Conrad.

The very simple-mindedness of the computer plays a significant part in its highly symbiotic relationship with humans. It is everything we are not. Human beings, by and large, are imaginative, intuitive, sensitive to values and occasionally capricious. A computer is none of these things. It can pay undivided attention to details that would drive a mortal right out of his mind. It can be told something and won't forget it until told to do so. It never gets huffy. It will work on the most boring problem forever without getting overheated. It will not laugh outright at human error and will work prodigiously at any problem put to it, no matter how trivial.

People who work with computers—especially those being exposed to a machine for the first time—can become quite entranced with these qualities, finding in the computer a kind of alter ego.

Sometimes programmers just won't go home, take a bath or anything [reports a computer man who has got over it himself]. They're like a kid falling in love with a hot rod. They'll sit there working with their newfound "friend" twenty hours a day, just watching the lights and drinking coffee. After a while they get to looking pale and unhealthy. They sit there fascinated and just forget to eat.

This affectionate relationship between man and machine takes its most acute form in major computer centers, where many people learning programming and using computers come together to work with one or a cluster of the big machines. Inevitably, the idea is to think up something new for the computer to do. Here both students and instructors devise rather fanciful programs that pit the machine's quick, literal and retentive mind against the inventiveness of humans. The results of such interaction can be quite impressive.

In one such center a game was devised with the program title of HR-3. When the operator typed in "HR-3," five rows of tiny lights, extending across the display console of the computer, were activated. In any given row a light would go on, then out, and the light to its right would be illuminated—and so on in all five rows from one side of the panel to the other. How fast the flashing lights moved across any row was determined by a program called a "random number generator," which has many uses in higher mathematics but was here employed to bump the lights along in random fashion. The group would bet on which row of lights would reach to the end of the console first. The winner bought morning coffee. What they had, with the aid of several million dollars' worth of computer, was a completely honest race, which accounts for the title of the program, "Horse Race 3."

A more complex program, which many centers worked out, involved teaching a computer to play blackjack. Anyone with access to the machine could type in the code word for the program, and the computer would type back:

WELCOME TO THE GAME OF BLACKJACK.

I AM GOING TO DEAL.

WHAT IS YOUR BET?

As the game progressed, the computer also kept a running tally of wins and losses, and would report this to any individual player even if he dialed a month later. A computer never forgets.

Such gambits are generally ill-regarded by the managers and bosses of computer centers—even if the purpose is training, computer time is still extremely expensive. It is said that a general in charge of one computer discovered the continuing blackjack game and ordered it erased from the computer's memory. This was obediently done. But the general didn't think to have the original program classified and burned, so it was surreptitiously put back in the machine— under a new heading in the program index. It may be there today, half forgotten among programs of great national import. Which brings up the fascinating (and quite real) possibility that someday an operator who wants the latest computerized estimate of China's nuclear capability—access Code BJ-20—will type into the machine instead BJ-21. And from the unforgetful machine will come the reply:

WELCOME TO THE GAME OF BLACKJACK.

I AM GOING TO DEAL.

## CAN MAN KEEP UP? [5]

Since the beginning of terrestrial history, man has been subject to nature. . . . [The year 1968] ended with a feat that symbolizes the central revolution of our time: man's growing control over nature. Men have for the first time sped beyond the gravity of this earth, looked down upon our distant, spinning globe and asked in sudden mockery if this planet harbored life.

This escape from the pull of the earth symbolizes a revolution in human life and consciousness as profound as any before it. The Copernican revolution removed man from the center of the universe, and the Darwinian revolution deprived him of his unique position as not-an-animal. Today the technological revolution is depriving man of both the security and the constraint that came from subjugation to nature in its given visible forms.

### Old Reins Are Off

Man is learning to understand the inner processes of nature, to intervene in them and to use his understanding for

[5] From article "Does Human Nature Change in a Technological Revolution," by Kenneth Keniston, professor of psychology at the Yale University Medical School. New York *Times*. p C 143. Ja. 6, '69. © 1969 by The New York Times Company. Reprinted by permission.

his own purposes, both destructive and benign. Increasingly, the old reins are off, and the limits (if any) of the future remain to be defined.

But what of man himself? Do the constraints of human nature still apply? How will the change in man's relationship to nature change man? No one can answer these questions with assurance, for the future of humanity is not predestined but created by human folly and wisdom. Yet what is already happening to modern men can provide some insight into our human future.

If there is any one fact that today unites all men in the world, it is adaptation to revolutionary change in every aspect of life—in society, in values, in technology, in politics and even in the shape of the physical world. In the underdeveloped world, just as in the industrialized nations, change has encroached upon every stable pattern of life, on all tribal and traditional values, on the structure and functions of the family and on the relations between the generations.

Furthermore, every index suggests that the rate of change will increase up to the as yet untested limits of human adaptability. Thus, man's relationship to his individual and collective past will increasingly be one of dislocation, of that peculiar mixture of freedom and loss that inevitably accompanies massive and relentless change.

As the relevance of the past decreases, the present—all that can be known and experienced in the here-and-now—will assume even greater importance. Similarly, the gap between the generations will grow, and each new generation will feel itself compelled to define anew what is meaningful, true, beautiful and relevant, instead of simply accepting the solutions of the past. Already today, the young cannot simply emulate the parental generation; tomorrow, they will feel even more obliged to criticize, analyze, and to reject, even as they attempt to re-create.

A second characteristic of modern man is the prolongation of psychological development. The burgeoning technology of the highly industrialized nations has enormously increased opportunities for education, has prolonged the postponement of adult responsibilities and has made possible an extraordinary continuation of emotional, intellectual and ethical growth for millions of children and adolescents.

In earlier eras, most men and women assumed adult responsibilities in childhood or at puberty.

## Prolonged Childhood

Today, in the advanced nations, mass education continues through the teens and for many, into the twenties. The extension of education, the postponement of adulthood, opens new possibilities to millions of young men and women for the development of a degree of emotional maturity, ethical commitment and intellectual sophistication that was once open only to a tiny minority. And in the future, as education is extended and prolonged, an ever larger part of the world population will have what Santayana praised as the advantages of a "prolonged childhood."

This will have two consequences. First, youth, disengaged from the adult world and allowed to question and challenge, can be counted on to provide an increasingly vociferous commentary on existing societies, their institutions and their values. Youthful unrest will be a continuing feature of the future.

Second, because of greater independence of thought, emotional maturity and ethical commitment, men and women will be more complex, more finely differentiated and psychologically integrated, more subtly attuned to their environments, more developed as people. Perhaps the greatest human accomplishment of the technological revolution will be the unfolding of human potentials heretofore suppressed.

Finally, in today's developed nations we see the emergence of new life styles and outlooks that can be summarized in the concept of technological man. Perhaps here the astronauts provide a portent of the future. Studies of the men who man the space capsules speak not of their valor, their dreams, or their ethical commitments, but of their "professionalism and feeling of craftsmanship," their concern "with the application of thought to problems solvable in terms of technical knowledge and professional experience," and their "respect for technical competence."

The ascendancy of technological man is of course bitterly resisted. The technological revolution creates technological man but it also creates two powerful reactions against the technological life style. On the one hand it creates, especially in youth, new humanist countercultures devoted to all that technological man minimizes: feeling, intensity of personal relationships, fantasy, the exploration and expansion of consciousness, the radical reform of existing institutions, the furtherance of human as opposed to purely technical values.

## Three-Way Contest

On the other hand, technological change creates reactionary counterforces among those whose skills, life-styles and values have been made obsolete. In the future, the struggle between these three orientations—technological, humanistic and reactionary—will inevitably continue. Technological man, like the technology he serves, is ethically neutral. The struggle for the social and political future will therefore be waged between those who seek to rehumanize technology and those who seek to return to a romanticized, pretechnological path.

Much of what will happen to men and women in the future is good—or if not good, then at least necessary. Yet it may not be good enough. The revolution over nature has already given men the capacity to destroy tenfold all of mankind, and that capacity will be vastly multiplied in the future. And many of the likely future characteristics of men—openness, fluidity, adaptability, professional competence, technical skill and the absence of passion—are essentially soulless qualities. They can equally be applied to committing genocide, to feeding the starving, to conquering space or to waging thermonuclear war.

Such qualities are truly virtuous only if guided by an ethic that makes central the preservation and unfolding of human life and that defines "man" as any citizen of this spinning globe. So far, the technological revolution has neither activated nor extended such an ethic.

Indeed, I sometimes feel that we detect no life on any of the myriad planets of other suns in distant galaxies for just this reason. I sometimes fear that creatures on other planets, having achieved control of nature but lacking an overriding devotion to life, ended by using their control of nature to destroy their life.

In this regard, the future of man remains profoundly uncertain.

## THE LIFELONG SCHOOL [6]

"We are now founding colleges at the rate of twenty or more a year," says Frank Bowles, one of the Ford Foundation's top education specialists. "I believe that within ten years we will be founding them at the rate of one a week."

And that only begins to suggest the magnitude of the growth and change American education will undergo in the next few decades.

Enrollments at all levels will soar. Census Bureau forecasts indicate the United States school-age population (five to twenty-four) will swell to more than 125 million by the year 2000 from 70.2 million in early 1967. The proportion of this group actually in the classroom will climb because of the surge in college undergraduate and graduate study. Moreover, the young people will be joined in the pursuit of education by rising numbers of adults.

The nature of instruction will change, too. The stress will be on flexibility. Students will move from lectures and demonstrations by master teachers in giant lecture halls to intimate seminar rooms to cubicles equipped with every sort of electronic teaching aid. Rigid class levels will disappear

[6] From "Shape of the Future: The Lifelong School," by Richard Martin. *Wall Street Journal.* p 1+. F. 13, '67. Reprinted by permission.

and students will advance at their own speed: a twelve-year-old might be an eighth grader in mathematics, a seventh grader in history and a sixth grader in English.

Computers will be the key to this individualized education. Teaching machines plugged into computers will drill youngsters in arithmetic, grammar and reading skills, grading them and correcting their mistakes instantly. Robert D. Tschirgi, dean of academic planning and professor of physiology and anatomy at the University of California's Berkeley campus, calls the computer "the greatest thing to hit education since Johann Gutenberg invented movable type."

Educational content as well as methods will change in fundamental fashion between now and the end of the century. Education authorities say this change will be forced by rapid technological developments that will outmode specific skills learned in the classroom. Curriculums will emphasize teaching not what the facts are but how students can gather the facts they need, analyze them and make decisions. Instead of swallowing a predigested textbook version of George Washington's role in American history, for example, students might be told to dig into several sources and come up with their own appraisal of his career.

"We simply can't continue to provide the facts needed to make decisions in a world where most of the facts we'll need are still unknown," says Nolan Estes, an official of the United States Office of Education.

By learning how to learn, people will fit themselves for the constant reeducation necessary if they are to continue to play useful roles in the economy, educators say. "We are in the early stages of a technological world that is going to require essentially all people to have to go to school continually to stay abreast of the changes," says Harold Clark, professor of educational economics at Columbia University's Teachers College.

This educational updating process, which will be carried on at work and in the home, often by electronic means, as well as in formal classrooms, is part of the explanation for the anticipated increase in adult education. But another factor in this increase will be expanded leisure, which is expected to lead to more demand for adult education unrelated to practical ends. Such a prospect causes one educator to wax eloquent. "In the world of 2000," he says, "we may look for a return to the ancient values of the pursuit of truth and beauty—of enlightenment for its own sake."

The increased demand for education of all types means that education will assume new importance in the economy. Salaries, construction and other expenditures for formal education now account for more than 6 per cent of the $739.5 billion gross national product. Some Office of Education officials estimate that such outlays will generate as much as 25 per cent of the $2.3 trillion GNP [gross national product] expected in 2000. How much expenditures for instruction outside regular classrooms will rise is anybody's guess, but the increase is sure to be immense.

"It is apparent that education will be the new dynamic of our national economy—that learning is the new growth industry," says Harold B. Gores, president of Educational Facilities Laboratories Incorporated, a nonprofit corporation established by the Ford Foundation.

That the Federal Government and industry will bulk larger in education in the future is accepted as certain even by educators who are uneasy about the trend, which promises to weaken their control over schooling. Federal officials insist the Government will remain a junior partner in education, concerned mainly with financing, and corporate executives say industry's function will continue to be to supply whatever educational materials teachers want. But it is clear both Government and industry will play increasingly active parts in deciding what schools will teach and how they will present it.

Litton Industries Incorporated, Burroughs Corporation and several other firms already are deeply involved in education through their operation of antipoverty Job Corps centers. A number of electronics companies and business machine makers have plunged into educational markets through mergers and acquisitions. The Government intends to use new educational research and development centers it is opening across the country to speed the introduction of new teaching techniques and equipment in schools.

This Federal effort to accelerate educational innovation, which is paralleled by prodding administered by private foundations in the form of pilot projects and demonstration grants, must contend with education's traditional resistance to change. "The aircraft industry would go out of business in two years if it changed as slowly as education," says Loyd Turner, president of the Fort Worth, Texas, school board and assistant to the president of General Dynamics Corporation.

But the innovators aim to break this pattern. One of their top-priority goals is to capitalize on the computer's capabilities in education.

The machines won't replace teachers. John Walton, chairman of Johns Hopkins University's education department, says they will be used "the same way totalizators are used at the race track to figure odds, payoffs and so forth. The heroes there are still the jockeys and horses, just as teachers and students will continue to be the heroes in the classroom while the gadgetry handles a lot of the drudgery."

The gadgetry still must be perfected, but no one doubts this will be done within the next few years. Manufacturers already have devised computer-run teaching machines that respond to spoken, written, typed or push-button questions and answer by flashing slides and movies on a screen, sending teletypewriter messages and even by talking back with pre-recorded vocabularies.

You can have a friendly relationship with a computer that a teacher couldn't find time for [says G. E. Callahan, educational marketing specialist with American Telephone and Telegraph Company]. It's never impatient, and the computer remembers exactly what each kid it is tutoring knows.

Computerized education will take place in the home as well as in the classroom. Youngsters will drill in basic subjects at home, guided by school computers linked to a teletypewriter or other types of outlets in the home. Library data-retrieval services and commercial home-learning courses will be available over the same sort of network. Tomorrow's encyclopedia might be sold as a subscription service that would give customers instant access to any piece of information stored by the encyclopedia publisher's computer.

Technological innovations in education won't be limited to computers. Overhead projectors that show close-ups of materials on the teacher's desk and enlarge microscopic views of laboratory experiments will supplement blackboards. Closed-circuit television and picture-phone communications will make lectures and demonstrations by outstanding teachers available to many students in classrooms across the nation simultaneously. Videotape presentations of everything from erupting volcanoes to historical skits will enliven instruction.

Advancing technology will greatly influence the design of tomorrow's schools. Logan Wilson, president of the American Council on Education, a professional organization, cautions that "before we begin to visualize strange egg-shaped structures in which students of 1984 may painlessly acquire knowledge, we might remind ourselves that a good deal of teaching still goes on in buildings erected before 1894."

But new schools, to a considerable extent, will have to be built around the electronic gear that will cram them. Moreover, the future schools will reflect the stress on flexibility in instruction, with sliding partitions and easily removable equipment permitting the use of space for many purposes. At the flip of a switch, for example, an auditorium might convert into a dozen small lecture halls.

Many planners predict that more and more communities will concentrate all levels of school facilities in centrally located "educational parks." This concept goes against the tradition of small neighborhood schools for elementary pupils and requires more transportation for youngsters. But advocates say educational parks will eliminate needless duplication of costly facilities and allow top teachers to reach larger numbers of pupils. They also see such consolidation as a way to end *de facto* school segregation and eliminate poor quality schools in slums and rural areas.

East Orange, New Jersey, plans to have its dozen city schools combined into a single "educational plaza" by 1980. Multistoried schools will cover much of the eighteen-acre campus, with playgrounds located on the roofs of some buildings. Big city educational parks might stack their schools in skyscrapers, planners suggest, while small communities might strive for settings resembling today's college campuses.

Most authorities think that within the next couple of decades compulsory public schooling will begin at age four and continue through the equivalent of two years of college. The introduction of compulsory post-high-school training means a vast expansion of junior colleges, often called community colleges. Some educators believe every town of 50,000 population will need at least one community college.

These institutions will prepare many students to take jobs at the end of two years. The schools will become a prime source of medical technicians, data-processing specialists, electronics repairmen and other specialists critically needed in a scientific, automated age. Community colleges also will provide the first two years of college for perhaps half of all those youngsters working for bachelor's degrees; these students will transfer to universities for the remaining two years.

Edmund J. Gleazer, Jr., director of the American Association of Junior Colleges, sees tomorrow's community colleges as "educational service stations," open year-round, seven days a week and late into the night. They would be places where adults could go to retrain and upgrade themselves for changing job needs and to learn just for personal satisfaction.

Faculties will include businessmen and technicians who teach part-time for "the personal sense of reward, plus a fair salary, and as a way to keep current in their own specialized fields," says Mr. Gleazer. Curriculums will "get away from the idea of fifty-minute classes, one-year courses and offer lots of short-term programs," he adds.

Mr. Gleazer expects all higher education gradually to "get away from the formalities we now have for entering and the great ritual of getting out." This will be necessary in a society where job requirements are changed rapidly by technological advances and where even college-trained specialists may find their skills made obsolete several times during their working years, many educators say. Mr. Gleazer argues that higher education must be opened up so someone can study, go out and work and still get back "into the stream again" without being blocked by credit requirements, prerequisites and other formalities.

Many universities are likely to drop their two lower years as a result of community college expansion. On the other hand, at many universities two years or more of graduate study in specialized fields may well become almost routine. Postgraduate universities to explore the frontiers of knowledge will spring up, too; Rockefeller University (formerly Rockefeller Institute), whose research facilities in New York City have been the scene of notable advances in medical research and natural sciences, is considered a forerunner of this type of postgraduate institution.

Some smaller private universities seem doomed by current trends. For many of them tuition from freshman and sophomore courses, which are highly standardized and taught to large groups, is the difference between balanced budgets and operating losses. In addition, says Milton S. Eisenhower, retired president of Johns Hopkins, "it is questionable whether private philanthropy will continue to support as many private institutions as it has up to now."

Essentially, say educators, the situation among United States universities is that the rich are getting richer—and the poor are getting relatively poorer. Prestigious private schools and big state universities are attracting disproportionately large shares of philanthropic and government funds, it's said, with the result that any smaller institutions lag ever further behind in caliber of staff and facilities.

Some educators are highly critical of this trend. They say it concentrates too much power and influence in a few universities and tends to create a sort of class system that stigmatizes many lesser-known schools and their graduates. They also say the uneven distribution of private and Federal largess is leading to the atrophying of many small institutions that could fulfill a useful function if given adequate help.

Earl J. McGrath, director of the Institute of Higher Education at Columbia University Teachers College, is particularly disturbed by the "elitist philosophy" that he says guides the distribution of massive Federal support to a clique of big-name universities:

> The hundreds of millions of Federal dollars for research flow primarily to a few universities and to a few departments within them, and often only to a select group within these departments. . . .

He estimates ten top schools (among them: Massachusetts Institute of Technology, Harvard and the University of California) soak up nearly 40 per cent of the funds. One hundred universities—out of a total of 1,100 four-year institutions in the United States—receive all but 10 per cent of the money.

This concentration of resources is expected to lead to more multiversities—the name coined by former University of California President Clark Kerr for immense institutions like the 87,000-student, nine-campus school he headed. At such huge institutions, there is always the danger that the students will feel they are reduced to mere ciphers; this mood is generally given at least part of the blame for the riots that rocked the Berkeley campus of the University of California.

But some educators say the impact of bigness can be eased by dividing the large schools into a number of relatively small, self-contained undergraduate colleges. This is the approach already being taken at such universities as Michigan State, Florida State and Rutgers, and other institutions are likely to follow suit.

Educators also say the electronic gear that will make possible individualized instruction in lower grades will serve the same function in universities, further lessening the impact of mammoth enrollments. In dormitory rooms equipped with picture phones, teletypewriters and perhaps facsimile reproducers, students will be able to watch videotaped lectures, summon up research data and follow computerized instruction in languages, sciences and other courses.

College enrollments are due to rise far faster than the school population generally. Undergraduate ranks are expected to reach 15 million to 20 million by 2000, up from 5.5 million in 1967. Graduate students are expected to number between 2 million and 2.5 million by the close of the century, compared with 520,000 in 1967.

The new classrooms and dormitories such enrollment growth will demand stagger the imagination. Economist Peter F. Drucker has calculated that to make room for the more than 9 million students who will be crowding into colleges and universities as early as 1975, the United States must add facilities equal to twice all the campus buildings erected since Harvard University opened its doors in 1636.

None of this takes into account the vast expansion of corporate programs for advanced education of their own employees. Xerox Corporation already runs "what amounts to an internal university," with nearly 4,500 employees enrolled this year, says Joseph C. Wilson, chairman. Many other companies have similarly extensive educational programs.

# BIBLIOGRAPHY

An asterisk (*) preceding a reference indicates that the article or a part of it has been reprinted in this book.

## BOOKS, PAMPHLETS AND DOCUMENTS

Adler, Irving. Thinking machines: a layman's introduction to logic, Boolean algebra and computers. Day. '61.

Bartee, T. C. Digital computer fundamentals. McGraw. '60.

Berkeley, E. C. The computer revolution. Doubleday. '62.

Berkeley, E. C. Symbolic logic and intelligent machines. Reinhold. '59.

Berkeley, E. C. and Wainwright, Lawrence. Computers; their operation and applications. Reinhold. '56.

Bernstein, Jeremy. The analytical engine: computers; past, present, and future. Random House. '64.

Booth, A. D. Automation and computing. Macmillan. '59.

*Cole, R. W. Introduction to computing. McGraw. '69.

Ferkiss, V. C. Technological man; the myth and the reality. Braziller. '69.

> Review article: Ideas, techniques and machines that put us about where God is, by E. E. Morison. New York Times Magazine. p 1+. Mr. 30, '69.

Fink, D. G. Computers and the human mind. Doubleday. '66.

Gardner, Martin. Logic machines and diagrams. McGraw. '58.

*General Electric Company. You and the computer; a student's guide. The Company. 570 Lexington Ave. New York 10022. '65.

*Gielow, F. C. Jr. Introducing . . . the computer. International Business Machines Corporation. Data Processing Division. 112 E. Post Rd. White Plains, N.Y. 10601. n.d.

Guilbaud, G. T. What is cybernetics? Criterion. '59.

Halacy, D. S. Computers; the machines we think with. Harper. '62.

Hilton, A. M. Logic, computing machines and automation. Spartan. '63.

*International Business Machines Corporation. The computer comes of age. The Corporation. Data Processing Division. 112 E. Post Rd. White Plains, N.Y. 10601. n.d.

*International Business Machines Corporation. Programming: words that move machines. The Corporation. Data Processing Division. 112 E. Post Rd. White Plains, N.Y. 10601. n.d.

214

Irwin, W. C. Digital computer principles. Van Nostrand. '60.

*Jacker, Corinne. Man, memory & machines; an introduction to cybernetics. Macmillan. '64.

Laurie, E. J. Computers and how they work; IBM 1620, IBM 1401. Southwestern. '63.

Leed, Jacob, ed. The computer & literary style. Kent State University Press. '66.

Martin, E. W. Jr. Electronic data processing; an introduction. Irwin. '61.

Morrison, Philip, and Morrison, Emily, eds. Charles Babbage and his calculating engines; selected writings. Dover. '61.

Sackman, Harold. Computers, system science, and evolving society. Wiley. '67.

Saxon, J. A. COBOL; a self-instructional manual. Prentice-Hall. '63.

*Servan-Schreiber, J.-J. The American challenge. Atheneum. '68.
      Excerpts: Harper's Magazine. 237:31-42. Jl. '68.

Stibitz, G. R. and Larrivee, J. A. Mathematics and computers. McGraw. '57.

Taube, Mortimer. Computers and common sense; the myth of thinking machines. Columbia University Press. '61.

*Thomas, Shirley. Computers: their history, present applications, and future. Holt. '65.

Von Neumann, John. The computer and the brain. Yale University Press. '58.

Vorwald, Alan and Clark, Frank. Computers! from sand table to electronic brain. McGraw. '61.

Wilkes, M. V. Automatic digital computers. Wiley. '56.

*Zagoria, Sam. Working with automation. (Seminar on Manpower Policy and Program. Proceedings) United States. Department of Labor. Manpower Administration. Washington, D.C. 20210. '67.
      Condensed transcript of the seminar held in Washington, D.C. Oct. 13, 1966.

PERIODICALS

Academy of Management Journal. 10:287-91. S. '67. Mathematics as a language, or conversation with a computer. B. E. Goetz.

Advanced Management Journal. 33:15-21. Ap. '68. Individual freedom in an age of automation. R. S. White.

Aerospace Technology. 21:26. Ag. 14, '67. Computers viewed as ripe for more creative usage.

Aerospace Technology. 21:52-3. O. 9, '67. Voice-controlled computer is teachable [Litton's Mellonics division system]. R. Lindsey.

America. 117:550-1. N. 11, '67. Priests' union threatens strike; computerized confessional. P. J. Laux.

American Aviation. 27:46+. F. '64. Computer speeds transatlantic flight planning. J. S. Murphy.

American City. 78:88-90. Ja. '63. Computer is a super slide rule: Detroit. C. L. Palmer and J. A. Fox.

American City. 84:152. My. '69. Traffic controller for any intersection; Santa Monica, Calif.

American City. 84:16. Je. '69. War against crime quickens; LEADS [law enforcement automated data system].

American Economic Review. 57:1117-30. D. '67. Technological change and the demand for computers [since 1955; United States]. G. C. Chow.

American Gas Journal. 192:32-3. Je. '65. Glossary of common computer terms.

Architectural Forum. 129:58-61. S. '68. Architecture and the computer. E. D. Teicholz.

Aviation Week & Space Technology. 80:230-3. Mr. 16, '64. Microcircuits add to computer capability.

Aviation Week & Space Technology. 88:21. Ja. 15, '68. Salute to the transistor. P. J. Klass.

Bankers Monthly. 85:22-5. Ag. '68. Status of computer software. J. A. Postley.

Broadcasting. 60:37. My. 29, '61. Automation proving lab; re-education fund to help displaced workers learn new skills and find new employment.

Bulletin of the Atomic Scientists. 23:12-18. N. '67. New technological era: a view from the law. H. P. Green.

*Bulletin of the Atomic Scientists. 25:4-6. Je. '69. The impact of automation on society. F. L. Bates.

Business Week. p 185-6. O. 14, '61. How a computer puts its answers into words.

Business Week. p 96. O. 21, '61. Common language for computers?

Business Week. p 47-8. Je. 1, '63. Computers take to prophecy.

Business Week. p 75-6+. Ag. 14, '65. How steel jobs are dwindling; technology's advance.

Business Week. p 132-4+. Ja. 15, '66. Computers play cops and robbers.

Business Week. p 164-6. My. 14, '66. Information becomes a hot item.

Business Week. p 78+. Je. 17, '67. Quick-access pool for world data.

Business Week. p 64-5+. My. 24, '69. A new industry's wild ride [special report].

Business Week. p 70-1. Jl. 5, '69. Job bank in a computer pays off and branches out.

Business Week. p 84+. Ag. 23, '69. Software giant goes commercial.

Changing Times. 22:41-5. N. '68. This is how computers work.

Chemical Week. 103:68-9. O. 12, '68. Coming: computers for all.

Christian Century. 84:874-6. Jl. 5, '67. Consultation on technology and human values. G. M. Schurr.

*Christian Science Monitor. p 9. Jl. 20, '67. Machines are "talking back." R. H. Bolt.

*Christian Science Monitor. p 9. Jl. 27, '67. Free enterprise can be even freer. Simon Ramo.

Computers and Automation. 10:23-4+. S. '61. Computers in the arts. J. A. Thie.

Computers and Automation. 12:20-2+. Ag.; 35-40 S. '63. Electronic computers and scientific research. S. M. Ulam.

Computers and Automation. 12:10-15. S.; 18-26. O. '63. Development of the computer market in Europe. W. K. de Bruijn and others.

    *Correction*: 13:2. Ap. 64.

Computers and Automation. 12:10-17. O. '63. Hybrid computation; what and why? A. E. Rogers.

Computers and Automation. 13:8-9. Ap. '64. Science, privacy, and freedom. A. F. Westin.

Computers and Automation. 13:28-9+. Ap. '64. Public image of computing. H. J. Bergstein.

Computers and Automation. 14:17-18+. My. '65. International impact of computers and automation. E. C. Berkeley.

Computers and Automation. 14:12-17. S. '65. Romance of good teaching and the time-shared computer. E. C. Berkeley.

Computers and Automation. 14:29-30. S. '65. Pictures of Mars developed by digital computer.

Computers and Automation. 15:14-17. Ap. '66. Science and the advanced society. C. P. Snow.

Computers and Automation. 15:24-7. Ap. '66. Humanities and the computer; some current research problems. E. A. Bowles.

Computers and Automation. 16:30-1+. F. '67. Fundamental concepts of programming languages. J. E. Sammet.

Computers and Automation. 16:28-35. Jl.; 10. S.; 10-12 N. '67. Computers and some moral questions.

Computers and Automation. 16:16-17. S. '67. Computer programming—the career of the future. P. C. Smith.

Computers and Automation. 17:27-8. Ja. '68. Jobs and careers in data processing; the changing nature of programming. P. S. Herwitz.

Data Processing Magazine. 8:20-6. Jl. '66. Computer and the law. S. P. Sims.

Data Processing Magazine. 9:22-6+. My. '67. New source of programmer talent—the visually handicapped. G. H. Clautice.

Data Processing Magazine. 9:28-9. Jl. '67. Programming languages. C. H. Reynolds.

Data Processing Magazine. 9:28-9. D. '67. Oregon schools use mobile, portable computers. C. B. S. Grant.

Data Processing Magazine. 10:62-3. Mr. '68. Future and desk-top computers. T. A. Peck.

Datamation. 12:33-4+. D. '66. Computer's public image; attitudes and misconceptions. R. S. Lee.

Dun's Review. 91:13+. My. '68. Checkless society. J. J. Reynolds.

Dun's Review and Modern Industry. 82:pt 2 116-18+. S. '63. Midget computers and other amazing machines are helping management get more value for the office dollar. H. E. Klein.

Dun's Review and Modern Industry. 83:51-2+. F. '64. Does automation require a new economy? interview with J. I. Snyder, Jr. T. R. Brooks.

Ebony. 22:127-9. Ag. '67. Unemployment among youth: the explosive statistic!

Economist. 201:690+. N. 18, '61. Where do we go from here?

Economist. 217:82. O. 2, '65. Computer lessons in Whitehall.

Economist. 217:978-9. N. 27, '65. Are you making micro-circuits? future could be grim for electronic companies that are not.

Economist. 224:666. Ag. 19, '67. Analogue uses.

Economist. 228:52-3. Ag. 10, '68. Could America's computer business get taken over?

Editor & Publisher. 99:54. D. 10, '66. How computer works.

Editor & Publisher. 101:13. O. 19, '68. Computer system tailors copy to desired length.

Education Digest. 33:14-17. Mr. '68. Computer-assisted instruction: prospects and problems. G. T. Gleason.

Electronics World. 81:63. My. '69. Redistribution of computer market is forecast.

Electronics World. 81:53. Je. '69. Communications system aids Ohio police in war on crime; LEADS [law enforcement automated data system].

Esquire. 71:100-3. Ja. '69. Computers on the brain. Martin Mayer.

Financial Executive. 33:56-61. O. '65. Information utilities. R. E. Sprague.

Financial World. 127:7+. My. 31, '67. For rent: electronic Merlins.

*Fortune. 69:100-11+. Mr.; 140-5+. Ap.; 112-16+. Je.; 70:124-6+. Ag.; 120-1+. O. '64. The boundless age of the computer. G. H. Burck.

Fortune. 69:146-7+. Ap. '64. Security is too important to be left to computers. F. X. Kane.

Fortune. 70:154-5+. Jl. '64. Machines Bull's computer crisis; France's proud business-machine firm. T. R. Bransten and S. H. Brown.

Fortune. 73:120-5+. Je. '66. In electronics, the big stakes ride on tiny chips; integrated circuits. Philip Siekman.

Fortune. 74:118-23+. S.; 138-43+. O. '66. I.B.M.'s $5,000,000 gamble. T. A. Wise.

*Fortune. 76:88-91+. Ag. '67. Computer time-sharing—everyman at the console. Jeremy Main.

Fortune. 79:189-90. F. '69. New era of innovation. Irving Kristol.

Fortune. 80:126-9+. O. '69. Computers can't solve everything. Tom Alexander.

Harper's Magazine. 204:54-60. Mr. '52. Little gadget with a large future. L. H. Engel.

Harper's Magazine. 227:24+. D. '63. Computer poetry or, Sob suddenly, the bongos are moving. F. P. Tullius.

Harper's Magazine. 228:96-9. Je. '64. Secret of Stonehenge. G. S. Hawkins.

Harper's Magazine. 231:134-7. S. '65. Understanding the new math? Darrell Huff.

Harvard Business Review. 42:109-20. Mr. '64. Buy by computer. J. S. Widing, Jr. and C. G. Diamond.

Harvard Business Review. 46:83-91. Ja. '68. The computer comes of age. N. J. Dean.

Harvard Business Review. 47:4-5+. Ja. '69. How to deal with resistance to change. P. R. Lawrence.

Harvard Business Review. 47:128-36. Mr. '69. Time sharing takes off. Brandt Allen.

Industrial and Labor Relations Review. 20:414-32. Ap. '67. Computer hiring of dock workers in the Port of New York. V. H. Jensen.

Inland Printer/American Lithographer. 159:56-8+. Je. '67. Computerized composition: progress and problems; interview with A. E. Gardner. P. J. Sampson.

Inland Printer/American Lithographer. 161:63+. S. '68. McCall may bounce printing signals via satellite.

Iron Age. 192:61. D. 19, '63. Automation is not a demon. R. H. Eshelman.

Iron Age. 200:24. Ag. 31, '67. Will Germany's EXAPT speak English?

Iron Age. 202:11. N. 14, '68. Optical memory system to store more computer data.

Journal of Business. 36:166-78. Ap. '63. Automation; technique, mystique, critique. R. A. Solo.

Life. 50:108-10+. Mr. 3, '61. Machines are taking over. W. R. Young.

*Life. 63:60-72. O. 27, '67. How the computer gets the answer. Robert Campbell.
   *Reprinted in this volume:* The eerie interface of man and machine. p 72.

Life. 65:52-4. N. 8, '68. Luminous art of the computer.

Management Review. 50:51-3. My. '61. Challenges of second industrial revolution. A. J. Goldberg.

Management Review. 52:4-15. Jl. '64. Computers and today's business.

Management Science. 14:661-81. Jl. '68. Technological change and learning in the computer industry. J. L. Barr and K. E. Knight.

Mental Hygiene. 52:276-83. Ap. '68. Technology and social change: choosing a near future. K. D. Shinbach.

Missiles and Rockets. 8:24-5. F. 27, '61. Computer key to space achievement. R. R. Williamson.

Missiles and Rockets. 14:22-4+. F. 3, '64. Microelectronics: special report [with editorial comment]. C. D. LaFond and others.

Monthly Labor Review. 85:139-44. F. '62. Labor-management policy committee report on automation.

Monthly Labor Review. 88:III-IV. F. '65. Manpower implications of technological change.

Monthly Labor Review. 90:36-41. O. '67. Adjusting manpower requirements to constant change.

Nation. 204:427-9. Ap. 3, '67. Old worlds to conquer; technology gap. Howe Martyn.

Nation. 205:549-50. N. 27, '67. Of, by and for the rich.

National Civic Review. 54:350-3. Jl. '65. Electronic solon; computer's massive memory discovers forgotten laws, helps modernize legislature's processes. E. W. Brydges.

National Civic Review. 54:366-7. Jl. '65. EDP [electronic data processing] in government, East and West.

Nation's Business. 50:40-1+. Ap. '62. Automation creates new jobs.

Nation's Business. 53:58-60+. S. '65. New look at how machines make jobs; what happens to workers when automation arrives?

New Republic. 151:10-12. S. 5, '64. Great unemployment fallacy. E. L. Dale, Jr.
   *Discussion:* 151:37-8. S. 19; 27-30. S. 26, '64.

New Republic. 157:21. Ag. 19, '67. Post office box; electronic dating services. Neal White.

New Republic. 158:8. Ja. 20, '68. Where are the jobless?

*New York Times. p 15. Ja. 24, '66. Automation panel agrees on report. D. R. Jones.

New York Times. p 137. Ja. 8, '68. U.S. spent $24 billion in '67 on research.

New York Times. p 137-43. Ja. 8, '68. New York Times survey of scientific and technical innovations.

New York Times. p 65. Ap. 15, '68. J. Diebold forms Diebold Institute for Public Policy Studies to deal with human and social implications of technological change.

New York Times. p 72. My. 26, '68. McLuhan theory linking social unrest and violence to technological development discussed.

New York Times. p 57. S. 29, '68. Computer designers press search for faster machines.

New York Times. p F 1+. N. 3, '68. Fourth computer generation crowds adolescent third. W. D. Smith.

*New York Times. p C 85. Ja. 6, '69. Computer business races on. W. D. Smith.

*New York Times. p C 140. Ja. 6, '69. For easy rapport between man and machine there's nothing quite like an analog computer. Robert Vichnevetsky.

*New York Times. p C 141+. Ja. 6, '69. The search for meaning amid change. Zbigniew Brzezinski.

*New York Times. p C 141+. Ja. 6, '69. Uneasy world gains power over destiny. G. T. Seaborg.

*New York Times. p C 143. Ja. 6, '69. Does human nature change in a technological revolution? Kenneth Keniston.

New York Times. p 1+. Ja. 18, '69. Study terms technology a boon to individualism. W. K. Stevens.

New York Times. p 61+. Ja. 21, '69. I.B.M. battle is joined; antitrust suit challenges the giant in world's fastest growing industry. W. D. Smith.

New York Times. p 24. Mr. 27, '69. Times plans a computer service to store and supply information.

New York Times. p F 1+. Ap. 12, '69. Legal trap is hurting computers. W. D. Smith.

*New York Times. p 36. Jl. 17, '69. Computers and controllers. C. C. Kraft.

New York Times Magazine. p 27+. Ap. 7, '63. Fallacies and facts about automation. V. R. Fuchs.

New York Times Magazine. p 16+. Mr. 22, '64. Automation: threat and promise. J. I. Snyder, Jr.

New York Times Magazine. p 48-9+. O. 24, '65. Automation is here to liberate us. Eric Hoffer.

*New York Times Magazine. p 44-5+. Ja. 8, '67. Don't tell it to the computer. Vance Packard.

New Yorker. 39:58-60+. O. 19; 54-6+. O. 26, '63. Profiles; computer: analytical engine. Jeremy Bernstein.

New Yorker. 43:20-2. Je. 24, '67. Robots: Unimation, inc., makers of Unimate industrial robot; interview. T. H. Lindbom.

New Yorker. 43:25-7. Ag. 19, '67. No nonsense; interview. C. P. Lecht.

Newsweek. 59:57. Ap. 2, '62. People machine.

Newsweek. 61:59. F. 18, '63. My doctor, the computer.

Newsweek. 63:76-7. Mr. 2, '64. Dial H for history.

Newsweek. 65:73-8+. Ja. 25, '65. Challenge of automation.

Newsweek. 65:112+. My. 10, '65. New math: does it really add up?

Newsweek. 69:84-5. Mr. 27, '67. Computermania; eastern Europe is beginning to click.

Newsweek. 70:38-40. O. 30. '67. Scandal of the century; rich and poor. Arnaud de Borchgrave.

Newsweek. 71:57. Ja. 29, '68. Where the brains are.

Newsweek. 72:68-70. Ag. 19, '68. Computers: the booming state of the art.

Office. 55:132-4. Ja. '62. Development of computing machines. H. D. Huskey.

Paper Trade Journal. 150:76-9. Ap. 25, '66. Hybrid computer; powerful tool for process problems. M. D. Harter and G. R. Smith.

Parents' Magazine. 41:68-9. S. '66. Mom and dad study the new math; course sponsored by PTA of Beaumont, Tex. J. L. Creswell.

Parks & Recreation. 2:22+. S. '67. Computer, ogre or tool? M. A. Jensen.

Parks & Recreation. 2:28+. S. '67. Riddle for tomorrow's world: how to lead a good life; excerpts from address. E. F. Zeigler.

Personnel Administration. 25:4-11. Mr. '62. Automation and human relations; some problems and predictions. B. J. Speroff.

Popular Electronics. 18:47-51+. Mr. '63. Littler than Lilliput; microminiature electronics. L. E. Garner, Jr.

Reader's Digest. 89:151-2. O. '66. Why parents can't add [excerpt from Son of the Great Society]. Art Buchwald.

*Saturday Evening Post. 238:32-6+. D. 18, '65. "I'm out of a job, I'm all through." B. H. Bagdikian.

Saturday Review. 44:42-3. Ap. 1, '61. Where is science taking us. R. E. Bellman.

Saturday Review. 46:44-5. Je. 1, '63. Computer as a botanist; a British experiment in artificial intelligence. W. T. Williams.

Saturday Review. 47:31-2. Ag. 29, '64. New horizons in economics. R. L. Heilbroner.

Saturday Review. 48:95. Ja. 2, '65. Storing sparks tomorrow [excerpt from Promise and challenge of the computer]. David Sarnoff.

Saturday Review. 50:21-3. Jl. 15, '67. Cybernetic age: an optimist's view. G. T. Seaborg.

Saturday Review. 51:50-4. Mr. 2, '68. Must we rewrite the Constitution to control technology? W. H. Ferry.
    *Reply.* 51:49-52. Ag. 3, '68. A. J. Topol.

Saturday Review. 51:8+. My. 11, '68. Romeo and Univac. A. C. VanDine.

Saturday Review. 52:69-70. My. 10, '69. Computer with the green eyeshade. R. L. Tobin.

Science. 139:1231-2+. Mr. 22, '63. Man-computer relationship [discussion]. D. L. Johnson and A. L. Kobler.

Science. 156:38-44. Ap. 7, '67. Pattern classification by adaptive machines. C. A. Rosen.

Science. 163:1065-6. Mr. 7, '69. Automatic identification and measurement of cells by computer. S. A. Rosenberg and others.

Science Digest. 55:69-73. My. '64. Information revolution. G. L. Haller.

Science Digest. 61:18-19. F. '67. Machine with the roving eye; pattern recognition, feedback control system.

Science Digest. 61:41-8+. F. '67. Computers today. S. L. Englebardt.

Science Digest. 62:73-4. D. '67. Thinking machine. Isaac Asimov.

Science Digest. 63:81-2. Ja. '68. Computerized physicals.

Science Digest. 63:89. Mr. '68. Talking computers. S. V. Jones.

Science Digest. 65:38-9. My. '69. Diagnosing disease by computer.

Science News. 93:494-5. My. 25, '68. Computer encoding of fingerprints.

Science News Letter. 79:234-5. Ap. 15, '61. Can computers think?

Science News Letter. 79:370. Je. 17, '61. Brain probe computers.

Science News Letter. 80:219. S. 30, '61. Computer plots storms.

Science News Letter. 81:11. Ja. 6, '62. Computers used to help diagnose heart disease.

Science News Letter. 82:121. Ag. 25, '62. USSR three years behind in electronic computers.

Science News Letter. 82:286. N. 3, '62. Computer analyzes men.

Science News Letter. 82:315. N. 17, '62. Computer mimics weather.

Science News Letter. 82:347. D. 1, '62. Compute trips to planets.

Science News Letter. 83:72. F. 2, '63. Computer grows clouds and produces rain.

Science News Letter. 85:342. My. 30, '64. Computers aid doctors.

Science News Letter. 86:120. Ag. 22, '64. Historic computer paper found after twenty years.

Science News Letter. 86:250-1. O. 17, '64. War of the computers: Nov. 3. D. F. Nolan.

Science News Letter. 86:297. N. 7, '64. Computer shows how Shelley aped Milton.

Scientific American. 211:100-8. Jl. '64. Computer experiments in chemistry. D. L. Bunker.

Scientific American. 217:102. S. '67. Technology and the Negro.

Senior Scholastic. 87:12-14. N. 11, '65. Automation and jobs.

Senior Scholastic. 89:4-7+. O. 7, '66. Computer age: how distorted the image?

Senior Scholastic. 91:6-9+. O. 26, '67. Automation, computers, and the decline and fall of work.

Senior Scholastic. 93:6-7+. S. 20, '68. Checklists of change: the have not nations.

Space World. F-8-68:30-1. Ag. '69. EAI computer aided success of Apollo docking operations.

Steel. 153:44-5. O. 14, '63. Automation cuts 40,000 jobs weekly. J. I. Snyder, Jr.

Steel. 154:51. F. 21, '64. Brain-sized computer now possible.

Steel. 158:43. F. 14, '66. LBJ's automation report sure to draw more fire.

Supervision. 25:4-5. O. '63. Essence of automation. W. C. Zinck.

Supervisory Management. 7:39-41. F. '62. What is a computer? J. R. Pierce.

Supervisory Management. 10:8-12. D. '65. Computers; new tool on the production line.

*Time. 59:57-9. F. 11, '52. The versatile midgets.

Time. 80:83-4. O. 19, '62. They're catching up; combining analogue and digital computers.

Time. 81:86+. Mr. 8, '63. IBM v. the others.

Time. 82:78. S. 6, '63. Brainy breed; annual conference of Association for Computing Machinery.

Time. 82:82. D. 13, '63. Automating the archives; computer to take over the lawyer's plodding search through archives.

Time. 83:53. Mr. 27, '64. Small memory for large numbers; ceramic memory units.

Time. 89:46. F. 24, '67. Extending man's grasp.

Time. 90:10. D. 29, '67. Employer of last resort [President Johnson's proposal].

Time. 91:19. F. 2, '68. Jobs for 500,000; Job opportunities in business sector.

Time. 92:50. Jl. 26, '68. Quick detective; ElectroCardioAnalyzer.

Today's Health. 39:22-5+. D. '61. How computers save babies' lives. K. N. Anderson.

Trans-Action. 5:20-7. S. '68. Computers, polls & public opinion. R. P. Abelson.

Trans-Action. 6:3-4+. Jl. '69. Poverty as underdevelopment. P. L. van den Berghe.

U.S. News & World Report. 54:88-9. Ap. 1, '63. When automation comes and workers stay on; Southern Pacific railway.

U.S. News & World Report. 56:80-4. F. 24, '64. Is the computer running wild?

U.S. News & World Report. 58:80-2. My. 10, '65. Myth of big-scale unemployment.

U.S. News & World Report. 61:82. D. 5, '66. Unemployed: a new definition.

U.S. News & World Report. 62:54-7. Je. 26, '67. What comes next in the computer age; interview. John Diebold.

*U.S. News & World Report. 65:54-7. Jl. 1, '68. Training the unemployables, Lockheed aircraft.

U.S. News & World Report. 66:84-5. Ap. 14, '69. When computer handles hiring.

UNESCO Courier. 19:22-9. Je. '66. Why 1101=13; new approaches to mathematics teaching. Nicole Picard.

Vital Speeches of the Day. 28:285-8. F. 15, '62. Computers and world leadership; address, December 12, 1961. D. L. Bibby.

Vital Speeches of the Day. 28:729-32. S. 15, '62. Impact of information processing on mankind; address, August 27, 1962. I. L. Auerbach.

Vital Speeches of the Day. 35:528-33. Je. 15, '69. Technology and society; the right to privacy; address, March 26, 1969. C. E. Gallagher.

Vogue. 140:194+. S. 15, '62. New brainwork in beauty; Univac electronic brain.

*Wall Street Journal. p 1+. F. 13, '67. Shape of the future: the lifelong school. Richard Martin.

Wall Street Journal. p 22. F. 13, '67. The librarian of tomorrow is likely to be a computer.

Wall Street Journal. p 1. Mr. 16, '67. Long distance teaching is tried between classrooms in Morehead, Ky., and a computer in California.

Wall Street Journal. p 1. Ap. 20, '67. Computer courses catch on at more liberal arts colleges.

Wall Street Journal. p 11. My. 5, '67. Gathering of weather data spurred in drive to program computers to control climate.

Wall Street Journal. p 1. Ag. 30, '67. New labor "brains": unions begin to use computers to prepare negotiating positions.

Wall Street Journal. p 16. N. 31, '67. Computer programming course to be taught at Sing Sing prison.

Wall Street Journal. p 1+. Ja. 10, '68. Telephone operators: ingenious young men outfox phone firms.

Wall Street Journal. p 8. F. 8, '68. Four students place class into computer to help job search.

*Wall Street Journal. p 1+. Ap. 5, '68. Whir, blink—jackpot! crooked operators use computers to embezzle money from companies. Alan Adelson.

Wall Street Journal. p 12. Ap. 16, '68. Computer seen as tool to aid scholars find forgeries, catalog art.

Wall Street Journal. p 7. Je. 13, '68. Computer-service started in New York to match unemployed quickly to job openings around country.

Wall Street Journal. p 10. D. 11, '68. Computerization process of designing cars seen as key in General Motors Corp.'s drive to keep selling price of new small car under $2,000.

*Wall Street Journal. p 1+. Ag. 11, '69. Compact computers. S. R. Schmedel.

Wall Street Journal. p 1. N. 14, '69. Computer room disasters set companies scrambling to protect precious files containing irreplaceable data.